WASHINGTON, D.C.

A Photographic Journey

TEXT: **Suzi Forbes**

CAPTIONS: **Fleur Robertson**

DESIGNED BY: **Teddy Hartshorn**

EDITORIAL: **Gill Waugh**

PRODUCTION: **Ruth Arthur and David Proffit**

DIRECTOR OF PRODUCTION: **Gerald Hughes**

DIRECTOR OF PUBLISHING: **David Gibbon**

CLB 2620
© 1990 Colour Library Books Ltd., Godalming, Surrey, England.
All rights reserved.
This 1996 edition is published by Crescent Books,
a division of Random House Value Publishing, Inc.,
40 Engelhard Avenue, Avenel, New Jersey 07001

Random House
New York • Toronto • London • Sydney • Auckland

Printed and bound in Malaysia

ISBN 0 517 05306 3

10 9 8

WASHINGTON, D.C.

A Photographic Journey

Text by
SUZI FORBES

CRESCENT BOOKS
NEW YORK · AVENEL, NEW JERSEY

If Ninian Beall could see his land grant today, he'd scarcely recognize it. Beall was a fighter – and that's in the literal sense. This tall, fiesty, red-headed Scot fought for Charles II of England. In the Battle of Dunbar, he was captured and sent to Barbados and then to a distant land called Maryland. There he was forced to work for no pay for five years.

When his period of indenture was over, probably between 1680 and 1685, he was given fifty acres of land. It was uncommonly lovely land but totally nonproductive. Nevertheless, Beall was grateful. He decided to make this place named Maryland his home and from that time forward his name loomed large in Chesapeake history. He held many public offices, became an Indian fighter, a planter, a grist-mill operator and owner of an iron foundry. But mostly he was a military man, fiercely loyal to his king in England, and, for each encounter he won for his country, Beall was given additional land grants. It is estimated that, over the years, he was given as much as 25,000 acres.

In 1687 he received a 1,503-acre plot that is now an integral part of the National Arboretum. We know he also owned a 255-acre tract called "Beall's Levels," where the White House now stands. His 795-acre plot, which he named "Rock of Dumbarton" after a Scottish landmark, was owned by his youngest son George when it was surveyed in 1752 for the new port town of Georgetown.

Beall was a fortunate man. The land he was given was extremely well-situated. It lies just where the foothills of the Appalachian Mountains roll down to meet the lowlands of the Tidewater, right at the highest point on the Potomac that a ship can travel. It combines a safe and protected harbor with a beautiful and harmonious site.

The Algonquin Indians had long loved this spot. They farmed its fertile soil, fished the abundant rivers, hunted the deer and buffalo that roamed the meadows and fashioned quartz knives and spearheads from the stone quarries found in Rock Creek. A traveller with a sharp eye can still find remnants of the Indian workshop where they chipped, flaked and polished their stones, in Rock Creek Park.

The first white man to extol the virtues of the Potomac River was Sir Walter Raleigh in 1585. He had heard of a land rich with animals, birds and fish where an Indian population who are "voyde of all covertouness lyve cherfullye and at their harts ease."

Raleigh hoped fervently to see this new land one day. He was enthralled with its opportunities. He secured substantial financial backing, charted a southerly route and sponsored two trips to America on his own. One member of the expedition, John White, came back with colorful paintings of the wildlife and Indians they found. This was enough to obtain backing for a third trip – this time to establish a colony. But alas, all members of that crew vanished from sight, leaving not a single trace. Nevertheless, Raleigh named the new land "Virginia," in honor of Elizabeth, the Virgin Queen.

In 1608 John Smith became the first Englishman to travel up the Potomac, saying to his crew, "Regain therefore your old spirits, for return I will not until I have found the Patawomeck." Two years earlier, at the age of twenty-seven, he had arrived in the New World with the first permanent English colonists. His inquiring mind and adventurous spirit wouldn't allow him to be content with farming. He was eager to learn all he could about his new country and to report his findings back to England. He became America's first explorer and the leader of his colony.

Smith was the first to locate the setting that would later become the Nation's capitol. A crew member said that the expedition was made "to search for a glistening metal the savages told us they had (taken) from Patawomeck, also to search what furs, and what other minerals, rivers, rock, nation, woods, fishings, victuals, and what other commodities the land afforded, and whether the bay were endless or how far it extended."

It was undoubtedly gold they sought but it's not what they found. Smith made detailed maps and his records were later used as a foundation for his General Historie of Virginia. His maps were later used in boundary decisions.

Of that first voyage, one of the crew members wrote, "Having gone so high as we could with the boat, we met divers savages in canoes, well loaded with the flesh of bears, deer and other beasts, whereof we had part. Here we found mighty rocks growing in some places above the ground as high as the shrubb, trees and divers other solid quarries of divers tinctures; and divers places where the waters had fallen from the high mountains, they had left a tinctured, spangled scurf that made many bare places seem as gilded." These were the quartz quarries.

Smith himself noted that it was the gold that brought men to Virginia. He said there was "no talke, no hope, nor worke, but dig gold, wash gold, refine gold, load gold." Yet they found no gold.

As the northern towns of Boston and New York established themselves as trading ports and merchant centers, life along the Potomac languished. John Smith's fledgling colony, located in Jamestown, Virginia, suffered from a lack of manpower in general and especially of men who were true leaders. For the most part, the first colonists were incompetent and mutinous or worse.

In 1607 a new wave of 600 settlers arrived but Smith sent critical letters back to England complaining about the selection. England had sent him craftsmen to make soap, glass, tar and candles. He pleaded with them to instead send him "but 30 Carpenters, husbandmen, gardiners, fishermen, blacksmiths, masons and diggers up of trees, roots... (rather) than a thousand of such as we have."

Recognizing the value of learning from the local Indians, Smith soon planted and began cultivating Indian corn. He despised the lazy shirkers in the colony and passed a rule in the spring of 1609 that food should be refused to those who didn't work for it. That seemed too autocratic to the rest of the colony, however, and Smith was replaced as head of the Virginia Company.

Lord Delaware took Smith's place and was also named Virginia's first governor. Disease, Indian attack and malnutrition continued to take their toll on the colony. Eventually there were a mere 60 settlers left. Who would have known at this bleak moment in history that survival and even prosperity lay just ahead.

One of the expeditions financed by Sir Walter Raleigh had brought back a leaf that England called a "sotweed." We know it as tobacco. It gained immediate, though disputed, acceptance. King James I wrote heatedly against it, but its popularity continued to grow. Raleigh even had the affrontery to puff a pipe of tobacco before ascending the scaffold for execution as a result of his continued conflicts with the crown.

In 1612 John Rolfe developed an effective method of curing tobacco that made shipment to England a possibility. And thus was born the young colony's first export trade. By 1619 it seemed clear that the Virginia Company would attain security and affluence.

No story of the young settlers in Virginia, especially in the company of John Rolfe and John Smith, would be complete without mention of Pocahontas, the lovely daughter of the Algonquin chief, Powhatan. It is said that fiesty John Smith was about to have his head chopped off when Pocahontas, then 12 years old, rushed to his defense and laid her head on top of Smith's to save him from certain death. Her act so moved her father that he spared Smith's life.

Historical accounts unanimously describe Pocahontas as gentle and beautiful. In Smith's Historie he says, "she next under God, was still the instrument to preserve this Colonie from death, famine and utter confusion." Never one to be accused of modesty, Smith was probably referring to his own deliverance, due to her intervention.

Pocahontas married John Rolfe (whose courtship of her inspired a tender poem by Henry Wadsworth Longfellow). Together they went to England to deliver personally Rolfe's first tobacco crop. They were an immediate success, as was their "sotweed" but, regrettably, Pocahontas died in England.

By the year 1630 the land surrounding the Potomac River was solely under the jurisdiction of Virginia. That would soon change. Lord Baltimore had been given a royal patent for Newfoundland. But be found it unbearably cold and wrote to King Charles I saying: "From the midst of October to the midst of May there is a sad face of winter upon all this land, both sea and land so frozen for the greatest part of the time as they are unpenetrable no plant or vegetable thing appearing out of the earth until it be about the beginning of May, nor fish in the sea besides the air so intollerable cold as it is hardly to be endured...

"I am determined to commit this place to

fishermen that are better able to encounter storms and hard weather, and to remove myself with some 40 persons to your Majesty's dominion of Virginia, where if your Majesty will please to grant me a precinct of land with such privileges as the King your father my gracious master was pleased to grant me here, I shall endeavour to the utmost of my power to deserve it and pray for your Majesty's long and happy reign..."

If King Charles had ever visited his subject in Newfoundland, he undoubtedly would have granted his request immediately. As it was, it took three years. But, as a reward for Baltimore's patience, Charles carved out a slice of Virginia in 1632. In gratitude, Baltimore named the new territory after Charles' wife, Henrietta Maria. Some maps identify it as Mariland and others as we know it today, Maryland.

Lord Baltimore's oldest son realized his father's dream of American colonization. He outfitted two ships, *The Ark* and *The Dove* and sent some 200 adventurers to colonize Maryland in 1634. Baltimore's men landed at St. Maries and immediately established a settlement. His liberal religious views led to Maryland's unique Act of Toleration in 1649.

Baltimore had converted to Catholicism shortly before he settled Maryland and he intended to make Maryland a sanctuary for other English Catholics who were being discriminated against. Since the majority of new arrivals to Maryland were Protestants, however, the Act of Toleration granted religious freedom to all persons who believed in Christianity. It was a unique piece of legislation, unlike any other in the New World.

Religious tolerance or not, however, the transition of power from one king to another in England had an unsettling effect on the fledgling colony. From the time of Henry VIII, the religious tolerance of England swayed with the religious persuasion of its ruler. When Protestant William and Mary ascended the English throne in 1689, they took back the province of Maryland from Baltimore and established the Church of England as the religion of the realm. They even moved the capitol from Catholic St. Maries to Protestant Anne Arundel (now called Annapolis).

As time passed, the fourth Lord Baltimore even became a convert to the Church of England himself and, with that, all doubt about the family's loyalty to the crown was dissipated. The family's proprietorship to the land was restored in 1715.

As late as 1678, the third Lord Baltimore wrote, "The principal place or town is called St. Maries, where the General Assemblies and provincial Court are kept, and whither all ships trading there doe in ye first place resort but it can hardly be called a town... there are not above 30 houses, and these at considerable distances from each other, and the buildings as in all other parts of the Province very mean and little, and generally after ye manner of the meanest farm houses in England."

Although the towns and the houses in Maryland may have been small and rustic, enterprising men were arriving on the scene at last who would bring success and prosperity. In 1632 an Englishman by the name of Henry Fleete arrived.

Fleete noted, "...we came to an anchor about two leagues short of the Falls, being the latitude 41, on the 26th of June. This place without all question is the most pleasant and heathfull place in all this Cuntry, and most convenient for habitacon, the aier temperate in somer and not violent in winter. It aboundeth with all manner of fishe... The Indians in one night... will catch 30 Sturgeons in a place of the river where it is not above 12 fadom broade; And as for deare Buffaloes, beares, and Turkies, the woods do swarm with them and the soil is exceedingly fertile."

Fleete noticed the Indians were careful to skin the bear and deer they caught but had no use for beaver, either to eat or for their pelts. Yet the fur of the beaver was to this Englishman's eye the most luxuriant and lovely of all. Therefore, he set up the first known beaver trade, arranging that "all the Indians... in the River of Patawomack will take paines this winter in the killinge of Beavers and preserve the furres for mee now that they beginne to finde what benefot it may accrew to them hereby."

Beaver hats became a mark of prosperity, with their tall crowns and wide brims showing off the soft, deep fur of the beaver to its best advantage. There were all the rage in England and Fleete soon found a ready market for his pelts.

And so, the adolescent community prospered. Planting was the primary trade, with tobacco the predominant crop.

In 1672, a Richard Blome reported, "...the general trade of Maryland depends chiefly upon Tobacco, which being esteemed better for a Foreign Market than that of Virginia, finds greater vent abroad; and the planters at home, in exchange thereof, are furnished by the Merchant with all necessaries, for himself, his House, Family and Plantation."

Virginia and Maryland practised an English

manorial system. Large estates, usually amounting to 1,000 acres or more, were called a "manor," with its owner addressed as a "lord."

The banks of the Potomac were gradually inhabited by the most aristocratic families in the new land. The Calverts, family name of Lord Baltimore's descendents, occupied as estate called Mount Airy near Mount Vernon. Thomas Notley and Ninian Beall were not far away, as were the Lees, Fairfaxes, Digges, the Addisons and the Washingtons.

Mount Vernon itself was granted to Nicholas Spencer and John Washington, the great-grandfather of George Washington, in 1674. No house was built there, however, until 1735. When that burned in 1739, the family moved away until 1743 when Lawrence Washington, George Washington's elder half-brother, built a house for his new bride. They lived there until 1752 when Lawrence died on a trip to Barbados. The house and property were left to his infant daughter, who died of consumption two years later and the property then passed to George Washington.

The social life of the planters was a genteel one. Tobacco had brought great wealth. There were few hotels, so every house welcomed travelers and guests. There was nothing unusual in riding some ten miles to pay a social call or to dine. George Washington once wrote that his family did not once sit down to dinner alone for 20 years. An abundance of slaves left ample leisure time.

Curiously, the slave trade actually began in New England, where no self-respecting landowner would own a slave, and it began in a most unlikely way.

It was a known fact that New Englanders liked their rum. They liked it so much that they started making it themselves. Why pay to have it imported all the way from England or Jamaica, they reasoned? Rum wasn't hard to make. All you needed was molasses. And once you had molasses, you could ferment and distill it into rum. But molasses is made from sugar cane, and sugar cane just didn't grow in New England. So those inventive folk in Newport, Rhode Island started a system known as the "Triangular Trade."

They would send their ships to the West Indies where sugar cane was plentiful, buy lots of molasses and bring it back to Newport. There, they would make it into rum, load some of it back on a ship and take it to Africa (they seem to have been partial to New England rum there.) They would then load the ship with slaves from Africa and take them to the West Indies, where they would be traded for molasses and then they'd return to New England. New Englanders didn't believe in slavery and certainly wouldn't have brought any slaves back to New England with them, but they grew very wealthy on the slave trade. Their scruples didn't extend that far.

John Rolfe reported the first shipment of negroes from Africa in 1619. He said, "About the last of August came in a Dutch man of warre that sold us twenty negars."

The English colonies didn't invent slavery. It had existed for nearly two centuries before the settlement of Virginia. Slave traders recognized the need in the new colonies for strong laborers and determined to meet that need. By the 1640s it had become the practice to sell imported blacks as servants for life. By the 1660s, there were statutes in Virginia and Maryland that gave slavery a hereditary legal status.

This lifelong indenture set black slaves apart from white slaves, who might arrive to serve a period of from five to ten years to pay off a debt and were then freed. The lifetime status of blacks was justified in legislatures by plantation owners who were convinced they needed an assured supply of labor able to stand the heat of an open field day in and day out. Africans were raised in the heat, they argued, so they were necessary for the prosperity of Virginia and the planters. Who could then have known the disastrous effect this reasoning would eventually have on America? Soon the hordes of negroes outnumbered whites in the Tidewater region.

With prosperity came more planters, as well as artisans, merchants and mechanics. By 1744, Annapolis was a thriving center and in 1749 the town of Alexandria, previously known as Hunting Creek Warehouse and then as Garrison's Landing, was founded. It took its name from John Alexander, who sold some 60 acres to create the town.

Alexandria was the perfect location for a thriving tobacco inspection station. Tobacco was increasingly profitable. It was brought to the inspection station along the great King's Highway that meandered its way from Williamsburg to New York, right through the heart of Alexandria. The tobacco was brought to market by wagon or in special horsedrawn rigs that rolled the barrels behind them, creating a smooth roadbed surface. It became known as the "rolling road."

George Washington assisted John West, Jr. in surveying the streets of Alexandria in 1749. It was laid out in a grid pattern, with cobblestone paving on the streets, and brick houses. The distinctive feature of Alexandria are its cozy, walled gardens in the rear of the houses. Most streets are tree-lined with the brick facades of the houses reaching the sidewalks.

By 1797 William Laughton Smith reported, "Alexandria is a considerable place of trade, is well situated on the river which is three-fourths of a mile wide. It... is now thriving rapidly; the situation of the Town, a capital one, a fine eminence, plain level, and bounded by a pretty range of hills, an excellent, safe and commodious harbour, a fine back country to it, will soon make it a very important post. Much business is done here; there are about 3,200 inhabitants; the houses principally of brick..."

By 1751, another tobacco inspection station had been built on the Maryland side of the River. This was called Georgetown, after Ninian Beall's youngest son, George, who then owned the land. Both Georgetown and Alexandria were convinced they would soon rival New York and Philadelphia as great seaport towns.

One interesting event that took place in early Alexandria was the forerunner of things to come. The French and the Indians were harassing the village from the west, so five Colonial Governors met at Carlyle House in 1755 to see what could be done. It was agreed that General Edward Braddock would mount an attack against the Indians. He crossed the Potomac and landed at "Braddock's Rock" in Foggy Bottom. From there he proceeded to Georgetown and then north, where he met with an ambush and was killed. It was a young George Washington who led the surviving troops to safety.

One of the last accounts we have from General Braddock was contained in a letter to a young lady in England written the night before he died. It contains his impressions of Georgetown, which he seems to have taken by storm.

"... never have I attended a more complete banquet, or met better dressed or better mannered people than I met on my arrival in George Town... The men are very large and gallant, while the ladies are the most beautiful that my eyes have ever looked upon... The habitations of these genial folk... are stately buildings that have no superiors in England, and the interior decorations are things of beauty... In fact, dear madam, I might sum up everything by declaring George Town is indescribably lovely and I am loath to leave it and its hospitable people." Too bad he did.

One can imagine the dilemma of Virginia and Maryland when advised of the excessive taxes imposed by King George III in England. Up to this point, their chief concern had been in raising tobacco and living the life of landed gentry, much as they would have in England. Unlike the northern states, which had more laborers, larger cities and crowded conditions, the South was still primarily a land of large estates and wealth and they were loyal to the hand that fed them.

True, fiery orators such as Patrick Henry argued cases against the crown in the Virginia legislature. In 1763, he charged that the king had, "from being the Father of his people, degenerated into a Tyrant," forfeiting thereby "all right to his subjects' Obedience." Later he furiously warned George III to remember the fates of Caesar and Charles I.

Yet it was Virginia that led the support of Massachusetts when the British blockaded the Port of Boston. In a series of Resolves passed at a meeting chaired by George Washington at Alexandria Courthouse on July 18, 1774, Virginia called on all colonies to send food and money to Boston and to appoint deputies to Congress "to concert a general and uniform Plan for the Defence and Preservation of our common Rights."

Even a moderate George Washington had had enough. "Shall we," he asked, "after this, whine and cry for relief, when we have already tried it in vain?" A mere two months later, the First Continental Congress met in Philadelphia. And so, for the first time, the thirteen colonies were united in presence and in purpose.

Washington was little affected by the hostilities of the Revolutionary War. They contributed men and supplies and, of course, leaders, but no battles took place on the soil of future Washington.

During the War, the Continental Congress became a nomadic body. Within a single year – 1777 – it met in Baltimore, Philadelphia, Lancaster and York. In 1783 they settled in at Philadelphia until a mutinous band of Continental soldiers accosted them, demanding overdue pay. They fled to Princeton, but it was soon evident that that town could not accommodate all of them. A permanent resting place was imperative.

The New York Advertiser on January 27, 1791, said it all, "Where will Congress find a resting place? They have led a kind of vagrant life ever since 1774 when they first met to oppose Great Britain. Every place they have taken to reside in has been made too hot to hold them; either the enemy would not let them stay, or people made a clamour because they were too far north or too far south, and oblige them to remove... We pity the poor Congress-men, thus kicked and cuffed about from post to pillar – where can they find a home?"

For a while it appeared that Philadelphia would be named the "Federal Town," and delegates met there in 1787 to draft the Constitution of the United States. Then New York City was called upon to be the location of the first meeting of Congress under the new Constitution in 1789. This didn't meet with everyone's approval but it did seem to be centrally located and transportation allowed relatively easy access.

In 1790 Congress took up the issue of a permanent resting place. Out of frustration, Philadelphia was given the nod for a decade from December 1790 to 1800. But that was a temporary measure only. Finally, through an artful compromise reached with the guidance of statesman Thomas Jefferson, enough votes were gained for the "Federal City" on the banks of the Potomac, in exchange for an agreement that the Federal government assume the war debts of the North.

At last the site of the Federal City had been agreed upon. The uniqueness of the Potomac site was exciting. Men could visualize a modern city rising to meet the needs of an agressive new government. Rather than squeezing governmental needs into existing streets and buildings in already old towns, this city would be planned specifically to meet the needs of the government.

To design the magnificent new capitol of a great new country a Frenchman by the name of Pierre Charles L'Enfant was chosen. President Washington had met the French-trained architect when L'Enfant joined the Corp of Engineers during the war.

L'Enfant pleaded with Washington for an opportunity to help shape this new city. In a letter dated 1789, he wrote, "Sir, the late determination of Congress to lay the foundation of a city which is to become the capital of this vast empire offers so great an occasion of acquiring reputation to whoever may be appointed to conduct the execution of the business that your Excellency will not be surprised that my ambition and the desire I have of becoming a useful citizen should lead me to wish a share in the undertaking.

"No nation had ever before the opportunity offered them of deliberately deciding on the spot where their Capital City should be fixed... the plan should be drawn on such a scale as to leave room for that aggrandizement and embellishment which the increase of the wealth of the nation will permit it to pursue at any period however remote."

Washington agreed that L'Enfant was eminently qualified for the task and appointed a commission of three citizens to oversee the work, with Thomas Jefferson providing a guiding hand.

L'Enfant was born in Paris in 1754, the son of an artisan in the Gobelins tapestry factory. He grew up in artistic surroundings and was trained as an architect and engineer.

At the age of 23, caught up in the American struggle for liberty from England, he joined a ship full of soldiers and guns for America. He served as a volunteer at his own expense, and was awarded a commission as captain of engineers.

In 1779 he sought and was granted a transfer from the campaign in the north to the southern campaign. A hot-blooded lad, he wanted to see the enemy up close. As it turned out, he saw them closer than he had bargained for. He was seriously wounded at Savannah and was taken to Charleston to recover. He related, "in my bed till January, 1780. My weak state of health did not permit me to work at the fortifications of Charleston, and when the enemy debarked, I was still obliged to use a crutch."

L'Enfant had few equals in America. He was regularly called upon to give advice on many artistic subjects. Lafayette asked him to paint a portrait of General Washington, which he did. He gave advice on a marble palace, a jewel, a solemn procession, a fortress, and even designed a new building in Philadelphia.

In 1783, with the war over, l'Enfant returned to France. One of his duties, on behalf of the new American government, was to design and have made an elegant insignia for the Society of the Cincinnati.

The Society of the Cincinnati is unique in America – actually in the world. It was founded in 1783 by former officers of the Revolutionary War to celebrate their success, to aid members and families in need and to perpetuate the distinction of their descendents. Every member is descended from a known and documented officer of the War and there can be only one active member representing each officer at a time. The right of succession attaches to the eldest son. Washington was the Society's first president.

L'Enfant chose elegant eagles for the insignia and had them ordered from the finest French artisans. With a total disregard for cost, L'Enfant had soon spent all his own rather meagre resources, as well as those given him by the American government for the insignia.

He was forced to return to America in 1784,

where Congress "Resolved that, in consideration of services rendered by Major L'Enfant, the general meeting make arrangement for advancing him the sum of one thousand five hundred and forty-eight dollars, being the amount of the loss incurred by him in the negotiation for a number of eagles, or orders, of the Cincinnati."

On L'Enfant's return, he undertook the commission of several important buildings, including the remodeling of one of the first of New York's City Halls. Because it was to be the first site of the new Congress, it was renamed Federal Hall.

L'Enfant tried to make the building characteristically American. He used American marble for the fireplaces in the Senate chamber and designed an eagle with thirteen arrows in its talons. Everything was in place by April 30, 1789 for the inauguration of George Washington as the first President of the United States. L'Enfant's building was called the most beautiful building in the country and crowds came to see it. Sadly, it was demolished in 1812. Federal Hall National Monument now stands roughly on the same site.

L'Enfant saw his design of the Federal City as one large in scope, with broad streets and avenues and beautiful views afforded by hills and valleys. He saw gardens and parks, fountains and monuments. He surveyed and mapped and surveyed some more. In March he sent his first general ideas to Washington, in June a more complete set of ideas with drawings and in August a final set of plans. It was the final set that was eventually adopted.

As to the location of the Capitol and the White House, L'Enfant gave them particular attention. He wrote, "After much... search for an eligible situation, prompted, as I may say, from a fear of being prejudiced in favor of a first opinion, I could discover no one so advantageously to greet the congressional building as is that on the west end of Jenkins Heights, which stands as a pedestal waiting for a monument... Some might, perhaps, require less labor to be made agreeable, but, after all assistance of arts, none ever would be made so grand." It's on this very spot that the capitol now stands.

For the White House, then referred to as the "Presidential Palace," L'Enfant chose a position some distance from the Capitol, to give it the "sumptuousness of a palace, the convenience of a house and the agreeableness of a country seat."

He entreated the President to accept his plan in its entirety as he felt it "must leave to posterity a grand idea of the patriotic interest which promoted it." And he pleaded with Washington to back him up if any sought to limit his grand scale. "I remain assured you will conceive it essential to pursue with dignity the operation of an undertaking of a magnitude so worthy of the concern of a grand empire... over whose progress the eyes of every other nation, envying the opportunity denied them, will stand judge." Very little opposition was expressed to the plan and many positively raved about it.

L'Enfant's dedication to the entirety of his plan left him with no room to compromise, however. He insisted that every boulevard, every garden and every monument should be placed exactly where he had intended. He also refused to acknowledge the existence of the commission Washington had appointed to oversee the project, even going so far as to refuse to allow them to see his plan until a system could somehow be devised to distribute it nationwide, allowing all citizens an opportunity to buy plots of land at the same time.

L'Enfant's nearsightedness was his downfall. One of the capital's chief landowners, Daniel Carroll, decided, despite all warnings, to build his home across what was to become New Jersey Avenue. Washington tried to reason with L'Enfant to solve the problem, "by yielding a little in the present instance; and it will always be found sound policy to conciliate the good-will rather than provoke the enmity of any man, where it can be accomplished without much difficulty, inconvenience or loss."

L'Enfant would have no part of it. On his own authority, he hired some laborers, went to the house and demolished it. Washington was furious. He wrote, "In future I must strictly enjoin you to touch no man's property without his consent, or the previous order of the Commissioners. Having the beauty and regularity of your plan only in view, you pursue it as if every person or thing were obliged to yield to it."

Jefferson, the great conciliator, met with L'Enfant to attempt to gain some measure of reason. L'Enfant would yield on no point. His plan must be carried out in its entirety, to the last, or he would not assist. It was with regret that Jefferson advised the Commissioners, "It having been found impracticable to employ Major L'Enfant in that degree of subordination which was lawful and proper, he has been notified that his services were at an end."

L'Enfant's days of glory were over. He was paid nothing for his great plan. Furthermore, he had not copyrighted it, so engravings were made without his name attached and from which he received no funds. His entreaties to Congress yielded nothing.

America's first professional architect, Benjamin Latrobe, said of L'Enfant, "Daily thro' the city stalks the picture of famine. L'Enfant and his dog. The plan of the city is probably his, though others claim it. It is not worth disputing about... He is too proud to receive any assistance, and it is very doubtful in what manner he subsists." He died in 1825 a virtual pauper.

Yet, eventually, L'Enfant had his day. In January, 1902, the "Park Commission," composed of Daniel H. Burnham, Charles F. Mc Kim, Augustus Saint-Gaudens and Frederick Law Olmsted, presented its report on the improvement of Washington. It concluded, "The original plan of the city of Washington, having stood the test of a century, has met universal approval. The departures from that plan are to be regretted, and wherever possible, remedied."

And then finally, in April 1909, in a ceremony in the rotunda of the Capitol, Pierre L'Enfant's ashes were placed in state on their way to a final resting place in Arlington Cemetery. Elihu Root, then Secretary of State said, "Few men can afford to wait a hundred years to be remembered. It is not a change in L'Enfant that brings us here. It is we who have changed, who have just become able to appreciate his work. And our tribute to him should be to continue his work."

L'Enfant's gift to his adopted nation is a grand city of wide boulevards, grassy malls and elegant buildings and monuments. The streets are a maze of grids, triangles, "circles," and diagonals, affording vistas that are the envy of other cities.

By 1800, the capital was moved from Philadelphia to the town they now called Washington, as planned. Folks who seriously called it a town were laughed at, however. Part of the Capitol had been erected and the President's House was underway but mostly there was nothing but swampy ruts for future roads, a dense forest and temporary laborers shacks. Governor Morris of New York noted "We want nothing here but houses, cellars, kitchens, well-informed men, amiable women and other trifles of this kind to make our city perfect... It is the very best city in the world for a future residence."

An English visitor in 1803 described it vividly:

"Well we got here from Baltimore early on Tuesday morning, having traveled the greatest part of the night... The first notice you have of this embryo London (or to be more in tone with the American modesty this embryo Rome) is a small stone between two stumps of trees upon which is inscribed "The boundary of the City." This is proper enough for you have got about two miles to go before you fall in with a single inhabitant to tell you so. Immediately upon leaving this stone you rise a hill and come upon a large plain... and then first see the Capitol, a ponderous unfinished mass of brick and stone... one or two brick buildings with corresponding sheds, half a dozen straggling houses or fragments of houses fill up the view till you get there which now being the highest ground gives you a complete command of the Potomack with both its branches, together with George Town – I can compare the site upon which the Capitol stands and about a mile in circumference to the top of a Quakers hat and rest of this imperial city comprised on its brim...

"After having got down into my brim there is a most noble raised road with foot paths on each side with a row of poplars... which last the whole way to the President's Palace – a distance of about a mile and three quarters. On this road the number of Citizens may amount to about fifty families. The Palace is... without any fence but a few broken rails upon which hang his excellency's stockings and shirts to dry and his maids blue petticoat – acting almost as wings to this stone building are two immense brick piles which contain the public offices such as Secretary of State, Treasury and post office.

"From here as you approach the Rock Creek you find a thicker settlement but it is not till you cross the creek and get to George Town which was meant as it were only to the Western suburbs to this magnificent country town. It is curious to observe that, in spite of all the government plans to force the population towards the center of the Town, it has uniformly resisted, and is now progressing in a contrary direction."

Anyone who has ever wondered about the strange polyglot of architectural styles in Washington is certainly justified in doing so. At the time George Washington became President there were no trained American architects. Competitions were held for the design of the Capitol and the Presidential Palace. Dr. William Thornton, a medical doctor, submitted the winning design for the Capitol. The competition for the Presidential Palace was won by a carpenter.

George Washington never pretended to know anything about architecture and relied heavily on Thomas Jefferson's good taste.

Of the competition for the Federal City's first and most important buildings, Benjamin Latrobe later said, "The plans of the public buildings were obtained by public advertisement offering a reward for that most approved by General Washington. General Washington knew how to give liberty to his country, but was wholly ignorant of art. It is therefore not to be wondered, that the design of a physician, who was very ignorant of architecture was adopted for the Capitol, and of a carpenter for the president's house. The latter is not even original, but a mutilated copy of a badly designed building near Dublin."

Latrobe's comments were nothing but sour grapes, of course. Of the designs submitted, that of Dr. Thornton was the finest. In fact, he was given an extra three months to complete his work since the Commission was singularly unimpressed with the other entries.

Dr. Thornton's design was praised by President Washington for its "grandeur, simplicity and beauty." Jefferson said that its design "captivated the eyes and judgment of all." Thornton, on the other hand, was concerned about his lack of formal education in architecture, as he would also be responsible for executing his building. He wrote that he "lamented not having studied architecture and resolved to attempt the grand undertaking (the Capitol) and study at the same time."

Thornton's wife once said of him, "His search after knowledge was perhaps too general, as it embraced almost every subject... he could have attained perfection in any art of science had he given up his mind solely to one pursuit – philosophy, politics, Finance, astronomy, medicine, Botany, Poetry, painting, religion, agriculture, in short, all subjects by turns occupied his active and indefatigable mind."

Due to Thornton's inexperience, Thomas Jefferson, who was now President, appointed Latrobe to the position of surveyor of public buildings in 1803. This included responsibility for construction of the Capitol. Now tempers would really flare! Thornton said of Latrobe:

"This Dutchman in taste, this monument builder,

This planner of grand steps and walls,

This falling-arch maker, this blunder-roof gilder,

Himself still an architect calls."

Then George Hadfield, a young architect who would later contribute several distinguished buildings of his own to the new capital's landscape, said of Thornton, "This premium (for the best design of the Capitol) was offered at a period when scarcely a professional architect was to be found in any of the United States; which is plainly to be seen in the pile of trash presented as designs for said building."

Hadfield offered the following advice. "The proper way to have built the Capitol was to have offered an adequate sum to the most eminent architect in any of the European cities, to furnish the design and working drawings, also a person of his own choice to superintend the work. In that case the Capitol would have been long ago completed and for half the sum that has been expended on the present wreck." It seems that literally everyone thought they could do better.

Nevertheless, grumbling and protests aside, the building program went forward. The cornerstone had been laid by George Washington in 1793. Finally, in November of 1800 the North Wing was sufficiently complete for Congress to meet there for the first time. By 1807 the South Wing was complete as well, giving both the Senate and the House their own meeting room. The two chambers were connected by a wooden walkway.

Meanwhile, work had begun on the Presidential Palace as well, but the contractor/builder, James Hoban, who won the competition for this building, collected his share of criticism, especially from Latrobe. "... The style he proposes," said Latrobe, "is exactly consistent with Hoban's pile – a litter of pigs worthy of the great sow it surrounds, and of the wild Irish boar, the father of her."

The White House was the first public building constructed in Washington, but even though work began during Washington's term it is the one building that can't boast "Washington Slept Here." It was not ready for occupancy until 1800, when John and Abigail Adams were the first to move in. Even then, it left much to be desired as a residency.

Prior to Abigail's arrival, John wrote to her that "You will form the best idea of it from inspection." He was undoubtedly afraid if she knew the house's actual condition, she would refuse to come. On spending his first night alone in the White House, he wrote her, "I pray heaven to bestow the best of blessings on this house and all that shall hereafter inhabit it. May none but honest and wise men rule under this roof."

After her arrival Abigail Adams wrote privately to her daughter that the rooms were drafty and cold. "The house is made habitable but there is not a single apartment finished... We have not the least fence, yard or other convenience, without, and the great unfinished audience-room (the East Room) I made a drying room of, to hang up the clothes in."

She soon changed her mind, however, because she later declared, "It is a beautiful spot, capable of every improvement, and the more I view it, the more I am delighted with it."

Thomas Jefferson was the first to spend an entire presidency in the new quarters. Jefferson thought the house much too large and scoffed that it was "big enough for two emperors, one Pope and the grand Lama." Nevertheless, he added pavilions on the east and west sides to enlarge it.

In 1803, the first of many structural problems became apparent when the East Room ceiling collapsed, almost on the head of Jefferson's young secretary, Meriwether Lewis. No wonder he volunteered to lead an expedition to explore a route to the West. Even bears wouldn't be that dangerous!

Jefferson took great delight in furnishing the White House "in the antique taste" with early French and American pieces.

When James Madison became President in 1809 he brought a new elegance to the White House. His wife, the "incomparable" Dolly Madison, had acquired a reputation for good taste.

And then the Redcoats were back. It was August of 1814 and the War of 1812 was raging. Rear Admiral Cockburn and his British troops took control of Washington. Cocky, arrogant and sure of himself, Cockburn stood in the speaker's chair of the Senate and cried, "Shall this harbor of Yankee democracy be burned?" He received a chorus of "ayes," as men set torch to books, draperies and furniture. A heavy rain that night extinguished the fire but the Capitol building lay in ruins.

Margaret Bayard Smith described the violent, savage scene, "50 men, sailors and marines were marched by an officer, silently thro' the avenue, each carrying a long pole to which was fixed a ball about the circumference of a large plate, – when arrived at the building, each man was stationed at a window, with his pole and machine of wild-fire against it, at the word of command, at the same instant the windows were broken and this wild-fire thrown in, so that an instantaneous conflagration took place and the whole building was wrapt in flames and smoke. The spectators stood in awful silence, the city was light and the

heavens reddened with the blaze!"

As to the rest of the city, Latrobe wrote, "A greater benefit could not have accrued to this city than the destruction of its principal buildings by the British. It has now acquired the confidence of its own inhabitants in its permanence, and everybody who could save a little money, is now employing it in building himself a house."

Latrobe was in charge of rebuilding the Capitol, and this time he was more genially disposed to its design. Perhaps he had grown used to its looks. He called it "... a most magnificent ruin." Under his direction, the Senate and House chambers were restored and he embellished the sandstone columns with an original corn cob and tobacco leaf pattern on the capitals. Yet his feud with Thornton never waned. He bragged to Jefferson that these capitals gained him "more applause from members of Congress... than all the Works of Magnitude that surrounded them."

By 1817 Latrobe had been replaced by the eminent Boston architect Charles Bulfinch, who now assumed the title of Architect of the Capitol. Under Bulfinch's able direction, the central portion linking the North and South wings was completed and he finished the dome, all according to Thornton's original design, although he did enlarge it.

The fire of 1814 had a disastrous affect on the White House as well. Not content with merely burning the inside, the outside received severe damage also. Dolly Madison, warned the British were coming, fled just as they arrived, but not before she stripped a valuable Gilbert Stuart painting of George Washington from its frame (she couldn't remove the frame from the wall) and tucked it under her arm, along with other important government documents. She even took time to take her parrot to the French minister for safekeeping.

The Madisons were never able to return to the White House. Instead, they first moved to the Octagon and then into a small house on Pennsylvania Avenue. The White House needed virtually a total restoration, which took place under the direction of its original architect, James Hoban. The sandstone walls were now painted white, giving the mansion its current name, although it wasn't until Theodore Roosevelt's term that it was officially named the White House.

James Monroe was the first President to reoccupy the White House, which he did in 1817. Congress appropriated $20,000 and with that Monroe purchased the furniture that now forms the nucleus of the current furnishings.

Official society in the Monroe administration was stately and formal. Mrs. E.F. Ellet's Court Circles of the Republic reported, "The court circle in Monroe's administration still had the aristocratic spirit and elevated tone which had characterized the previous administrations. Its superiority was universally acknowledged, and nothing vulgar entered its precincts. Elegance of dress was absolutely required. On one occasion Mr. Monroe refused admission to a near relative who happened not to have a suit of small-clothes and silk hose in which to present himself at a public reception... The female society at Washington during the administration of Monroe was essentially Southern. Virginia, proud of her presidents, sent forth her brightest flowers to adorn the court circle. The wealth of the sugar and cotton planters, and of the vast wheatfields of the agricultural States, cultivated by negroes, enabled Southern Senators and Representatives to keep their carriages and liveried servants, and to maintain great state. Dinners and suppers with rich wines and the delicacies of the season, had their persuasive influence over the minds as well as the appetites of the entertained."

By 1820, President's Square facing the White House, (renamed Lafayette Square in 1824 in honor of the great General's return visit) was finally taking on a character of its own. St. John's Church had been constructed in 1816 and is still one of the finest examples of early American architecture. Latrobe was the architect and its first organist as well. For this project, because it was so close to his heart, he donated his architectural services.

Across the square, Decatur House was completed in 1819. Stephen Decatur was a dashing, daring military hero, who had fought in hand-to-hand combat against the Barbary pirates and the British during the War of 1812. New York was home to Decatur and his beautiful wife Susan, but when he was appointed to the board of navy commissioners, they moved to Washington and Decatur purchased a lot on President's Square for their new home.

Once again, Latrobe was selected as the architect. He built a three-story brick townhouse of lasting beauty. The Decaturs took possession in 1819. The first great party they gave in their new home was in honor of President Monroe's daughter, who was the first to be married in the White House.

Yet their happiness was shortlived. Merely fourteen months after moving into their grand new home, Decatur was killed in a duel. Unable to meet expenses, Susan Decatur moved to Georgetown and rented the house out. A series of distinguished tenants occupied it over the years, including two French ministers and three secretaries of state. These included Henry Clay, Martin Van Buren and Edward Livingstone.

In 1871 Decatur House was purchased by one of the most colorful figures to have graced Washington society. Edward Fitzgerald Beale was the man who, in 1848, had raced across the country from California to Washington to announce that gold had been discovered in California. Later, in one of his more interesting adventures, he persuaded Secretary of War Jefferson Davis to import camels from the Near East for use in the southwestern desert instead of mules. Two paintings currently hanging in Decatur House "The Search for Water" and "The Horses Eagerly Quenching Thirst, Camels Disdaining" were painted to commemorate that experiment.

Decatur house remained in the Beale family until 1956, when it was bequeathed to the National Trust for Historic Preservation. It's now one of the most interesting museum houses open to the public.

Not on Lafayette Square, but nearby on New York Avenue and Eighteenth Street, was one of the first private houses built in the new capital, Octagon House. George Washington had convinced his friend Col. John Tayloe III that the Federal City would soon be the London of the new world. He should build his new town house here rather than in Philadelphia.

In this case, Thornton was selected to design a house on the oddly shaped lot. His solution was ingenious. When it was finished in 1801, it was one of only three brick houses in the city. It was probably the most elegant, especially when the furnishings of Chippendale, Sheraton and Hepplewhite, all imported from England, were in place.

It seems that from the beginning, the Tayloes rented out their house for at least a portion of the year. During the War of 1812, it was leased to the French Minister and used as the French Embassy. With the French flag flying over the mansion, it was spared any damage.

When the French minister moved out a month after the White House burned, Tayloe invited the Madisons to take up residence. They gratefully accepted. No sooner had they moved in than Dolly resumed her lavish parties. The great men of the day were entertained at Octagon House and it was in President Madison's second floor study that the Treaty of Ghent, which ended the War, was signed.

The Tayloe family continued to occupy Octagon House until 1855 but then it fell on hard times. It served variously as a girls' school, government offices and finally a boarding house. When the American Institute of Architects leased the building in 1899, they found four feet of trash in the drawing room, fireplaces that were boarded up, broken windows, peeling paint and falling plaster.

No better tenant could have been found, however. They purchased the building in 1902 and began a restoration program that continues today. The Octagon House stands as one of the finest examples of true historic preservation in America. It is open to the public.

The era of elegant society was drawing to an end, ushered out by the Jackson administration in 1829. The first commoner was merely a "brawler from Tennessee," according to John Quincy Adams. But Andrew Jackson was more. He was a handsome frontiersman, the first President to have been born in a log cabin and the first proponent of a true democracy.

"Democracy" meant an end to the old school of wigs, ruffles, knee breeches and silver buckles. Jackson invited one and all to attend his inauguration – and they did. An eye witness account described it thus:

"The whole of the preceding day, immense crowds were coming into the city from all parts, lodgings could not be obtained, and the new comers had to go to George Town, which soon overflowed and others had to go to Alexandria... A national salute was fired early in the morning, and ushered in the 4th of March. By ten o'clock the avenue was crowded with carriages of every description, from splendid Barronet and coach, down to waggons and carts, filled with women and children, some in finery and some in rags... The day was warm and delightful, from the South Terrace we had a view of Pennsylvania and Louisiana Avenues, crowded with people hurrying towards the Capitol... At the moment the General entered the portico and advanced to the table, the shout that rent the air still resounds in my ears. When the speech was over, and the President made his parting bow, the barrier that had separated the people from him was broken down and they rushed up the steps all eager to shake hands with him. It was with difficulty he made his way through the Capitol and down the hill to the gateway that opens on the avenue. Here for a moment he was stopped. The living mass was impenetrable. After a while a passage was opened, and he mounted his horse which had been provided for his return. Then such a cortege as followed him! Country men, farmers, gentlemen, mounted and dismounted, boys, women and children, black and white. Carriages, waggons and carts all pursuing him to the President's House."

As the first President truly "of the people", Jackson invited the "people" into the White House for the reception following his oath-taking. They clambered on the furniture in muddy boots, smashed china and glassware, tore draperies from the windows, knocked waiters off their feet and caused a tremendous commotion. Jackson himself finally escaped through an open window.

As to the agreeableness of the Federal City by now, opinions varied widely. A French visitor, the Chevalier de Bacourt, was horrified by what he saw. "I went to see Mr. and Mrs. Charles Hill, who live at the extreme end of the city; my carriage sank up to the axle-tree in the snow and mud; it was necessary to leave the carriage, which had to be dragged out and scraped to remove the mud and slush which stuck to it like glue. I don't know how anyone can get to the Hill's on Monday next, when they give a ball; they count on the moon shining that night to save their necks...

"The nights are so noisy that one can scarcely sleep. There is a continual uproar, the reason for which is that the inhabitants all own cows and pigs, but no stables, and these animals wander about all day and all night through the city, and go to their owners' houses only in the morning and evening to be fed; the women milk their cows on the sidewalk and sprinkle the passersby. The nocturnal wanderings of these beasts create an infernal racket, in which they are joined by dogs and cats."

Frances Trollope, on the other hand, positively rhapsodized during a visit in 1831. "I was delighted with the whole aspect of Washington; light, cheerful, and airy, it reminded me of our fashionable watering-places (in England). It has been laughed at by foreigners, and even by natives, because the original plan of the city was upon an enormous scale, and but a very small part of it has been as yet executed. But I confess I see nothing in the least degree ridiculous about it; the original design, which was as beautiful as it was extensive, has been in no way departed from, and all that has been done has been done well.

"From the base of the hill on which the Capitol stands extends a street of most magnificent width, planted on each side with trees, and ornamented by many splendid shops. This street, which is called Pennsylvania Avenue, is above a mile in length, and at the end of it is the handsome mansion of the president; conveniently near to his residence are the various public offices all handsome, simple, and commodious; ample areas are left round each, where grass and shrubs refresh the eye. In another of the principal streets is the general post office, and not far from it is a very noble townhall. Towards the quarter of the president's house are several handsome dwellings, which are chiefly occupied by the foreign ministers.

"The houses in the other parts of the city are scattered, but without ever losing sight of the regularity of the original plan; and to a person who has been traveling much through the country, and marked the immense quantity of new manufactories, new canals, new rail-roads, new towns, and new cities, which are springing, as it were, from the earth in every part of it, the appearance of the metropolis rising gradually into life and splendour, is a spectacle of high historic interest."

And things were improving. In 1835 the Baltimore and Ohio Railroad completed its tracks between Washington and Baltimore and began service with four trains daily. Men could make the trip in a mere two hours, compared to at least four by stagecoach. In 1840 the population of Washington had increased to 44,000 and by 1850 it had climbed to 51,700.

Even so, Frances Trollope may have been exaggerating Washington's progress, because twenty years later, in 1852, Charles Dickens said of Washington: "It is sometimes called the City of Magnificent Distances, but it might with greater propriety be termed the City of Magnificent Intentions; for it is only on taking a bird's-eye view of it from the top of the Capitol that one can at all comprehend the vast designs of its projector, an aspiring Frenchman. Spacious avenues, that begin in nothing, and lead nowhere; streets, milelong, that only want houses, roads, and inhabitants, public buildings that need but a public to be complete... are its leading features. One might fancy the season over, and most of the houses gone out of town forever, with their masters." To him, Washington was a "monument raised to a deceased project."

And yet, culture had certainly come to Washington. As early as 1800 the first theater opened in Blodgett's Hotel. Even though several opera presentations, accompanied by a 20-piece orchestra and several theatrical productions, were staged, the theater was not a resounding success. It closed a month after it opened. But the Washington Theater, opening in 1804, had a longer career.

When the National Theater opened in 1835, however, Washington had its first truly fine theater. Operas, such a Mozart's *Marriage of Figaro* and Rossini's *Barber of Seville* were performed there, as well as legitimate plays. The National is still serving up fine theater.

Musical recitals, orchestral concerts, opera, theater and band music occupied the cultural life of Washington in the 1860s. Even Jenny Lind, the "Swedish Nightingale" came to town to "wow" Congress.

In 1798 Congress created the Marine Band, who conducted their first White House "musick" on New Year's Day 1801 for President John Adams. The New Year's White House concerts continued for years.

Ford's theater opened in 1861, under the name of Christy's Opera House. Its name was changed in 1863, after undergoing reconstruction following a fire.

If Washington was not growing as rapidly as George Washington originally thought it would, the rest of the country was undergoing tremendous expansion. By 1850 there were 31 states with a total population of 23,191,876 and a land mass equaling 2,992,620 square miles. There were 62 senators and 232 representatives all clamoring for space in the now diminutive Capitol. Something had to be done. Finally, Congress appropriated $100,000 to create "ample accommodations for the two houses of Congress."

This time it was a Philadelphia architect by the name of Thomas U. Walter who was in charge of the building. Walter's design suggestion had included a much larger dome, which Congress had also approved. So, the smaller, copper dome of Thornton's design, executed by Bulfinch, was removed and replaced by a mammoth 285-foot-high Baroque dome modeled after the ones topping the Pantheon and the Invalides in Paris. He executed it in a new technique, using nine million pounds of cast iron because it was fireproof and stronger, lighter and more versatile than stone.

And yet, just as construction began, so did a

tremendous feeling of unrest. The slavery issue had been boiling and subsiding in Washington for years. A predominantly Southern town, its sympathies were with slavery. Yet, as the seat of the Federal government, it found itself in a dilemmma. Congress outlawed the slave trade – but not slavery – in 1850. And just in time!

John Randolph of Roanoke reported, "In no part of the earth – not even excepting the rivers on the Coast of Africa, was there so great, so infamous a slave market, as in the metropolis, in the seat of government of this nation which prides itself on freedom."

The mood of the nation was turning positively ugly and the brewing volcano separating North and South was about to erupt. In 1858, William Yancy of Alabama said, "We shall fire the Southern heart – instruct the Southern mind... and at the proper moment, by one organized concerted action, we can precipitate the Cotton States into a revolution."

At the Democratic Convention, held in 1860 in Charleston, George Pugh of Ohio angrily declared, "The Northern Democrats are not children... we are told, in effect, that we must put our hands in our mouths, and our mouths in the dust. Gentlemen of the South, you mistake us – You mistake us! We will not do it!"

The Republicans fared no better. Abraham Lincoln was selected by his party to represent them. The South rumbled and swore they would not recognize a Republican President, but few Northerners took them seriously. Nevertheless, when Lincoln was elected, the Southern states knew what they must do. Between November, 1860 when the election took place and February, seven Deep South states voted to secede.

The secession question was most difficult for Virginia. They were not among the first states to secede and even called for a peace conference in Washington in February. Twenty-one states attended, but they failed to reach a compromise.

Lincoln's inaugural address gave the first clue to the greatness of the man elected to lead the nation. He specifically stated the government would act to defend itself, but cautioned the South, "In your hands, my dissatisfied fellow countrymen, and not in mine, is the momentous issue of civil war. The government will not assail you. You can have no conflict, without being yourself the aggressors. You have no oath registered in Heaven to destroy the government, while I shall have the most solemn one to 'preserve, protect and defend it.'"

Lincoln ended by saying: "I am loath to close. We are not enemies, but friends. We must not be enemies. Though passion may have strained, it must not break our bonds of affection. The mystic chords of memory, stretching from every battlefield, and patriot grave, to every living heart and hearthstone, all over this broad land, will yet swell the chorus of the Union, when again touched, as surely they will be, by the better angels of our nature."

But the brave words had little effect. Passions ran too high. The North had garrisoned men at Fort Sumpter, just offshore from Charleston. They were running short of supplies and Lincoln notified the government of South Carolina he was sending ships to replenish the supplies. But the Confederate government decided to take Fort Sumpter themselves before the supplies could arrive. On April 12, 1861, Confederate guns opened fire on Fort Sumpter. The fort surrendered the next day and the nation found itself at war.

Washington became the primary embarkation point for troops and supplies. The first major battle of the war, Bull Run, in July 1861, took place nearby and resulted in a resounding defeat for the Union troops. Suddenly, it became clear that if Washington were to survive, a series of forts must be built to defend the city.

Walt Whitman recorded the scene after the battle, "During the forenoon Washington gets all over motley with these defeated soldiers – queer looking objects, strange eyes and faces drenched (the steady rain drizzles on all day) and fearfully worn, hungry, haggard, blister'd in the feet. Good people... hurry up something for their grub. They put wash kettles on the fire, for soup, for coffee. They set tables on the sidewalks – wagon-loads of bread are purchas'd, swiftly cut in stout chunks..."

Fortifications were set up outside the city consisting of four batteries of heavy artillery and twenty-three light artillery batteries. They formed "a connected system of fortifications in which every point at intervals of 800-1000 yards was occupied by an enclosed field fort." If viewed from a hotel window at the center of town, it appeared the city was fully enclosed by a circle of camp fires.

Viewing this scene herself, Julia Ward Howe was inspired to write "The Battle Hymn of the Republic."

"I have seen Him in the watch fires of a hundred circling camps; They have builded Him an altar in the evening dews and damps..."

But even the Civil War failed to stop

construction on the new Capitol dome and wings. Said Lincoln, "If the people see the Capitol going on it is a sign we intend the Union shall go on."

Inside the Capitol things were far from normal. It became a barracks for as many as three thousand troops, who referred to it as the "Big Tent." In the basement, committee rooms were transformed into a bakery producing hundreds of loaves of bread for the army every day. The Capitol even served as a temporary hospital for soldiers wounded at the front, with cots lining the rotunda, halls and meeting rooms. The poet Walt Whitman, writer Louisa May Alcott and Red Cross founder Clara Barton were among those who administered to the sick and wounded.

The use of the Capitol by troops fighting for the Union had a lasting and positive effect on citizens. As writer Mary Clemmer Ames wrote, "How many an American boy, marching to its defense, beholding for the first time the great dome of the Capitol rising before his eyes, comprehended in one deep gaze, as he never had in his whole life before, all that the Capitol meant to him and to every free man... 'Washington City'... was no longer a name to the mother waiting and praying in the distant hamlet; her boy was camped on the floor of the rotunda. No longer a far off myth to the lonely wife; her husband held guard on the heights defending the capital. No longer a place food for nothing but political schemes to the village sage; his boy, wrapped in a blanket, slept on the stone steps of the great treasury.

"Never, till that hour, did the Federal city become to the heart of the American people what it had so long been in the eyes of the world – truly the capital of the nation."

Lincoln won re-election in 1864 and finally there was peace. In April, 1865 General Robert E. Lee surrendered his Southern forces to the North. The nation breathed a sigh of relief, little realizing the tremendous suffering the South would continue to endure.

At home in Washington, merely five days after Lee's surrender, Lincoln finally felt free to relax – at least for a few hours. On the night of April 14th, the President and Mrs. Lincoln attended a play at Ford's theatre. He had told her just that morning, "I never felt so happy in my life." And yet, during the play, John Wilkes Booth slipped into the Presidential box, leveled a derringer at Lincoln's head and fired. Lincoln died the next morning.

A Georgetown resident remembered the effect of the assassination, "The next morning we were notified by a delegation of negroes that unless we immediately festooned our house with crepe, the house would be attacked and our family imprisoned... It was impossible to purchase crepe or evidence of mourning, the demand being so much greater than the supply, and we had to resort to tearing up some of mother's old dark clothing, in order to use the same as mourning emblems. Every house was draped, and all were required to show at least outward sorrow. Later on we learned to appreciate the fact that in the death of Mr. Lincoln, the truly great man, the South and her people had lost a good friend; one whose kindly heart would have spared them many of the sufferings and tyrannies they were subsequently obliged to undergo as a result of his death."

Now it was time for the capital to forget and rebuild. Nowhere did the symbol of the reunited nation have more meaning than in Washington – especially in the Capitol building itself. The country took pride in seeing the work that had been accomplished during the war years.

The massive new dome had been completed and folks searched for the appropriate embellishment. A statue, affixed to the highest point, could be seen from afar. The American sculptor Thomas Crawford received the commission. He sketched a nineteen-and-one-half-foot tall bronze figure that he called "Armed Freedom." He placed a helmet on her head complete with an eagle head and feathers. She carries a sheathed sword in her right hand and a shield in her left.

She was hoisted to the top following a tumultous birth. The plaster case was modeled in the Rome studio of Crawford and placed aboard a ship bound for the United States in 1858. Buffeted by wind and storms, the ship could travel no further than Bermuda, where it was sold. The statue was placed in storage until it could be brought to the United States and finally cast in bronze.

"Freedom" was finally hoisted to the top in 1863. She has been hit by lightning many times and is now grounded by ten platinum-topped lightning rods. Even her platform is not that secure. In 1865, it was determined that the heat of the sun and subsequent cooling off at night make the dome orbit as much as three to four inches every day. Yet "Freedom" tenaciously hangs on!

Inside the new dome, which rises from the floor an astounding 180 feet and has a diameter of 100 feet, Presidents, starting with Lincoln, have lain in state and dignitaries have been received here with great ceremony.

The rotunda is noteworthy for its eight monumental paintings, especially those by John Trumbull, an aide-de-camp to George Washington during the Revolutionary War. His paintings were done from sketches he made as an eyewitness to the events. They include "The Declaration of Independence," "The Surrender of General Burgoyne," The Surrender of Lord Cornwallis," and "Washington Resigning His Commission as General of the Army." The realistic details include likenesses of actual participants. Trumbull received the princely sum of $8,000 for each of these paintings – a great deal of money at the time.

Another remarkable artistic work may be seen high inside the dome, and it has a remarkable story as well. Constantine Brumidi came to the United States from Italy in search of political freedom. An artist, he was familiar with fresco painting, the same technique used by Michelangelo in the Vatican's Sistine Chapel. The technique requires that paint be applied to fresh plaster, with the artist working quickly before the plaster dries.

Brumidi wanted "to make beautiful the Capitol of the one country on earth in which there is liberty." He devoted fully twenty-five years of his life to just that. In 1865, when he was sixty years old, he completed "The Apotheosis of Washington." To do so, he worked from a scaffold high above the ground. His work depicts Washington seated between Liberty and Victory. There are thirteen figures crowned with stars to represent the thirteen original colonies.

Not satisfied with the dome painting, he next started on a frieze that encircles the rotunda. While painting a scene from Willian Penn's treaty with the Indians in 1879, the artist, now seventy-four years old, slipped from the scaffolding. Incredibly, he managed to hang on until help arrived, but nevertheless died a few months later. A good portion of the frieze was completed by Filippo Costaggini – at least all but a thirty-foot panel. That was finally completed in 1953 by Allyn Cox.

During Brumidi's remarkable twenty-five year love affair with the nation's Capitol, he also embellished the Senate reception room, a corridor on the Senate side of the building, committee rooms and the President's Room. His beautiful medallions, birds, flowers, landscapes and patriotic motifs are a loving reminder of a man who loved liberty.

With the completion of the new House and Senate wings in 1857 and 1859, the ornate – even sumptuous – Old Senate Chamber, once the scene of fiery speeches by Calhoun, Clay and Webster, became the Supreme Court. The Court remained in these rich surroundings until 1935.

Mary Clemmer Ames used to watch the Court in session, "Here Clay, and Webster and Calhoun – those giants of the past... once held high conclave. Defiance and defeat, battle and triumph, argument and oratory, wisdom and folly once held here their court. It is now the chamber of peace. Tangled questions concerning life, liberty and the pursuit of personal happiness are still argued within these walls, but never in tones which would drown the sound of a dropping pin...

"In the Court room itself we seem to have reached an atmosphere where it is always afternoon. The door swings to and fro noiselessly, at the pull of the usher's string. The spectators move over a velvet carpet, which sends back no echo, to their velvet-cushioned seats ranged against the outer-walls. A single lawyer arguing some constitutional question, drones on within the railed inclosure of the Court; or a single judge in measured tones mumbles over the pages of his learned decision in some case long drawn out. Unless you are deeply interested in it, you will not stay long. The atmosphere is too soporific, you soon weary of absolute silence and decorum, and depart."

The old House of Representatives chamber, in constant use from 1807 to 1857, became Statuary Hall once the new chambers were complete. In 1864 Congress invited each state to send statues of two of its most favored sons. Unfortunately, it was realized by the 1930s that all that bronze and marble was just too heavy for the delicate chamber floor. Some statues remain but others are dispersed throughout the Capitol.

The Library of Congress had consistently been housed in the Capitol building overlooking the Mall. Congressmen would regularly send aides running down the hall to collect a book they needed to illustrate a point in their oratory. But it was also bulging at the seams.

It had been started in 1800 with a purchase of 3,000 books in London. These were destroyed in the fire of 1814, but when Thomas Jefferson sold his library of 6,000 volumes to the United States government, the Library of Congress was in business again. An expansion of the space within the Capitol was authorized but neighboring office occupants refused to vacate. Therefore, a competition was held for a new building in 1873.

In that same year General Lew Wallace, author of *Ben Hur*, could hardly contain his enthusiasm for the Library. He wrote to a family member that "the library grows visibly."

"Books, books – a mountain of books! How very delightful to sit among them, and lift your eyes from page or picture to the alcoves and balconies stories in height, and follow the shelves extending into dim perspective! How the gold lettering on the ground of scarlet and green illuminates the shadow and seems to people the silences. How intuitively visitors, entering the charmed space, uncover their heads, and move across the tileing on tiptoe and speak in whispers! 250,000 volumes! What labor they represent, and what laborers, the thinkers of all lettered times, and of all nations! They overflow the walls.

"A new building is projected. Sixty plans are already submitted by as many architects. (There were actually about twenty-seven.) The site chosen is the northwest corner of the garden adjoining the Capitol. Think of a building four stories, a quadrangle 400 feet on each side, in the centre a circular reading room 100 feet in diameter, from which in all directions the deep alcoves radiate – a building to hold 3,000,000 volumes. Such is the design!"

The Library of Congress far exceeds Wallace's expectations. Completed in 1897, this repository of over 80 million items is more than a library. It is also a museum and showplace of American art.

Over fifteen kinds of marble decorate the interior. Famed artists, such as Daniel Chester French and Augustus Saint-Gaudens, created sculptures to adorn it. A marble mosaic in the center of the main hall is actually a sunburst and compass, with polished brass rays pointing to brass zodiac signs. There are grand marble staircases, a soaring domed central hall that rises 125 feet, a stained glass skylight and countless paintings.

Not everyone was pleased with the design, however. Russell Sturgis, in 1898, had a complaint. He hated, "That false idea of grandeur which consists mainly in hoisting a building up from a reasonable level of the ground, mainly in order to secure for it a monstrous flight of steps..."

Inside the Library, the collection is incredible in its scope. There's a perfect vellum-printed Gutenberg Bible from 1455, the world's largest collection of comic books, 3.5 million pieces of sheet music, the largest collections of Chinese and Russian books outside those countries, Jefferson's rough draft of the Declaration of Independence,

five Stradivarius violins, 1,500 flutes, an extensive photography and print collection and much more. Even with all this, there are 400 more items added every hour.

The Library is still technically a part of Congress and is funded through the Legislative budget, but it's available to the public as well. Questions such as "How many artichokes are grown in California each year?" and "Why do you never see baby pigeons on the street?" are regularly asked of the staff of the Congressional Research Service. They'll prepare studies on request about law, history, economics, you name it. In fact, they get 2,000 requests a day.

The original building, completed in 1897, was long ago outgrown. The Adams Building was added in 1939 and the Madison Building in 1980. All are connected by underground passages, with book conveyors that speed the delivery of books while they protect them from the elements. But be prepared to literally move in, for an extensive research project, because books may not be removed from the library.

As for the rest of the city, the ravages of war left their mark, but at last something was about to be done. In 1870 it was said, "The surrounding forts, deserted now, were crumbling into decay, and the shedlike corrals for army horses and wagons were abandoned to the town toughs, who found them a convenient rendevous."

And then Alexander Shepherd came to the rescue. He was determined to see some improvements and, in 1870, he had just been made a member of the board of public works. By 1873, he was Governor of the District of Columbia. "With Czarlike zeal, he tore up the tracks of the railroad which crossed Pennsylvania Avenue at the foot of Capitol Hill near the Peace Monument. Before the dew was off the grass in the morning, he supervised the tearing down of the old Northern Liberties Market House on the square where the Carnegie Public Library now stands. One Saturday night, he nearly buried the depot of the Baltimore and Ohio Railroad at the corner of New Jersey Avenue and C Street by building up the street preparatory to grading and surfacing it." All of this was according to George Rothwell Brown, in *Washington: A Not too Serious History*.

When he'd finished demolishing, he began to build again. First, he laid miles and miles of sewers, paved the streets, put in sidewalks, increased the water supply, installed gas lamps along the streets and created parks. He even planted trees to line his newly paved streets.

A report by a Congressional committee said, "In three years the Board of Public Works, under the initiative and guidance of Shepherd and in the face of vigorous and weighty opposition, performed a work of such marvelous magnitude in the way of public improvements as to re-create the city, cause all agitation for the removal of the Capital to cease and make possible the new Washington of today. In these brief three years, under the controlling genius of this man, public works were accomplished of such magnitude as under ordinary circumstances would have required at least half a century."

But the improvements didn't come without a price—an enormous one. Some accused Shepherd of graft. All knew he had bankrupted the Capital. On a budget of $10,000,000, he had spent $22,000,000. He was eventually forced to flee to Mexico, with Congress assuming payment of the debt.

What he left behind was a permanent legacy. *The Graphic* in 1875 reported: "The improvements in the District of Columbia within a few years have been marked. Its broad and elegant avenues and parks and drives in all directions, its splended public buildings and rapidly increasing number of fine dwellings, its climate, libraries, society, and direct connection with all parts of the country, combine to make it one of the most attractive cities on the continent. People who remember it as it was in the old days before the war can hardly believe that it has been transformed into the new and elegant city of to-day."

By 1880 a reporter for *The Century Magazine* wrote, "Within the past ten years Washington has ceased to be a village. Whether it has yet become a city depends on 'the point of view.' It has no elevated railroads, no palace hotels, no mammoth elevators, no great commercial establishments; it has no opera and but indifferent theaters, and for a park it borrows the grounds of the old soldiers of the army... On the other hand it has large public buildings and monuments and numerous statues; it has a mild climate, clean, well paved streets and no 'local politics.' Its chief inhabitants are those persons who guide the action and control the interests of fifty millions of people... Washington is thus a place quite out of the ordinary run; whether city or no, it is certainly unlike other cities."

Journalist Frank Carpenter wrote, "The great charm of society in Washington is that it is not entirely founded on wealth. Its principal interest comes from the fact that the most important and successful men in all branches of activity come here. Instead of there being one lion to roar at a party, there may be ten or twenty or thirty. So many men and women of brains and brilliance give Washington gatherings a sparkle that is found nowhere else, except perhaps in the capitals of Europe. There is a frankness and a lack of snobbishness as regards wealth and fashion.

He also noted, "Washington seldom bothers itself about the skeletons in the inhabitant's closets. Lucifer himself will be welcomed if he will dress well, keep his hoofs hidden in patent leathers, and his tail out of sight."

Way back when L'Enfant devised his master plan for the Federal City he had laid out a splendid mall that extended from the Capitol west toward the Potomac River. This was intended as a public park with gardens for walking and diplomatic mansions lining its borders. He saw it as a "Grand Avenue, 400 feet in breadth... bordered with gardens, ending in a slope from the houses on each side."

He also planned a second mall extending from the White House to the Potomac. Where they intersected, L'Enfant planned a glorious monument to President Washington. Forgotten for fifty years, as other more pressing building projects took shape, the Mall plan was resurrected in the 1850s.

President Fillmore selected Andrew Jackson Downing to put order and turf to the swampy area that extended west. Two streams that had meandered through the area had already been diverted into a canal, all according to L'Enfant's plan. The canal served as a means of transportation.

The canal seemed to work well for a while because *The National Intelligencer* in 1815 reported that "Marble, stone, etc., are now landed at the foot of the Capitol which otherwise must have been hauled at a great expense from four times the distance. The citizens can now land everything near their doors with considerable reduction of expense, trouble and time."

But as early as 1826 it was apparent the canal was of little long-term use. It needed frequent dredging, was not deep enough for most boats and actually impeded cross-town land traffic. Eventually, the canal was condemned as a health hazard and in the early 1870s it was covered over altogether. The only remnant of the Washington Canal is the street that continues to bear its name. Nevertheless, it was an element Downing had to contend with in his plans for the Mall in 1850.

Actually, it's amazing there was still room for a Mall at all. In George Washington's will of 1795, he expressed his deep desire to see a national university constructed along the banks of the Washington Canal. He designated shares of canal stock for this express purpose.

Washington abhorred the practice of sending bright young men to Europe to learn. He felt, "... that a serious danger is encountered by sending abroad among other political systems those, who have not well learned the value of their own."

Adhering to Washington's wishes, plans for a national university along the Canal were drawn up in 1816. Fortunately, the value of the canal stock was worthless before the university could be built.

Another prior development that Downing would work around was the first building of the Smithsonian Institution. This crenelated, castle-like structure – still known as the "Castle," had been built in 1847 on the highest point of land in the Mall, in order to avoid the swampy marshes surrounding it. In fact, as a proper setting for the new Smithsonian, it gave the development of the Mall the impetus it needed.

Downing designed a tangled bower, filled with curling pathways and trees. It was to embody "the beauty of curved lines and natural groups of trees." Even then, however, it was intended that the Mall would end at the Washington Monument.

And what about the Washington Monument, that cornerstone of L'Enfant's plan? Well, as early as 1832, Congress appropriated money for a statue of Washington. L'Enfant had been specific in his details. He said it must be an equestrian statue of Washington and it must be of monumental proportions. Horacio Greenough was selected to do the work.

Frank Carpenter in the Cleveland Leader wrote, "It took eight years for Horatio Greenough to make (the statue). He did the work in Florence, Italy, where he chiseled out the Father of our Country in a sitting posture instead of standing, as the Act of Congress demanded.

"When the statue was completed, in 1840, the next question was how to get it from Italy to America. Congress haggled over the matter for weeks, finally sending a man-of-war to bring the statue across the Atlantic Ocean. But the marble George weighed twelve tons, and it took twenty-two yoke of oxen to haul him over the Italian roads...

"When it arrived at the Washington Navy Yard, Congressmen were horrified to see that our great hero had been carved sitting in a chair, nude to the waist. The Virginia statesman General Henry A. Wise remarked at the time. 'The man does not live, and never did live, who saw Washington without his shirt.'...

"At the Capitol doors, it was found that the statue was too large... The masonry had to be cut away and the door enlarged. When it was finally installed, the Rotunda floor began to sink, so a pedestal was built under it to support it. It was soon decided that the Rotunda was not a suitable place for the statue, and at last, after a number of removals, it was taken to... the bitter cold, bleak air of the Capitol plateau...

"One jokester, commenting on the outstretched sword in the figure's hand, says he is sure Washington is crying, 'Take my sword if you will, but bring me some clothes!'" The statue is now in the National Museum of American History, where at least it's out of the rain.

Perhaps foreseeing disaster, a Washington National Monument Society had been formed as early as 1833. They raised money from public subscription and sponsored a design competition. This time the location for the monument to Washington was planned where L'Enfant had visualized it originally – in the Mall.

The competition was won by Robert Mills, who designed a 600-foot obelisk that was to rise from a collonaded temple, itself 100 feet tall. The whole would rise to a height of 700 feet. The cornerstone was laid in 1848.

Money was still being raised and, to help with the costs, and to further immortalize the monument, states and countries donated marble blocks. By 1854, the monument had risen to 152 feet, but then it stopped.

In March of that year, Pope Pius IX sent a block of marble from Rome's Temple of Concord to be added to the Washington Monument. This infuriated the American Party, otherwise known as the Know-Nothings. They "stole" the whole monument by taking the Monument Society's records and electing their own members to the offices.

This aggressive act caused the termination of public and Congressional funding. And so, for twenty-five years, a useless half-finished spike stood as a reminder of what might have been. The stump in the middle of the Mall prompted Mark Twain to brand it "a factory chimney with the top broken off." It was a disastrous embarrassment! From 1855 to 1880, the monument was raised only four feet by the Know-Nothings and the masonry used was so poor that it had to be torn down later.

Finally, work got under way again, this time aided by a remarkable new contraption called an elevator to hoist workers and equipment to the top – and visitors too, when it was completed. *Harper's Weekly* in 1884 said, "The visitor will be seized upon by the genius of steam, and raised in a few moments in a comfortable elevator almost to the copper apex at its top.

"No one can examine this remarkable column without feeling that a new advance has been made in architecture... Why should we not have houses as tall? Why abandon the upper regions of the air and cling so closely to the tainted earth?"

And so, very slowly, the Mall that we know today came into being. Another huge step forward occurred in 1902, when Senator James McMillan authorized a Park Commission composed of the greats of the day: architect Daniel H. Burnham, landscape designer Frederick Law Olmsted, Jr., architect Charles F. McKim and sculptor Augustus Saint-Gaudens. Their charge was not merely to devise a new design for the Mall but to guide the future growth of Washington.

From the beginning, this esteemed group approached the task with energy and scholarship. They visited Rome, Venice, Vienna, Budapest, Paris and London. Their plan was far-reaching and effective. They were especially concerned that there be "fields for the populace." They suggested that the remaining Civil War forts be made into public parks, connected by a Fort Drive.

Most of all, their impact has been felt by their plan to extend the Mall beyond the Washington Monument. They specifically called for a monument dedicated to the memory of President Lincoln at its far end, connected to the Washington Monument by a canal, which later became the reflecting pool. To accomplish this, it was necessary to dredge and build up the area through landfills. Once complete, rows of elms were planted along the banks of the reflecting pool.

For the Lincoln Memorial, the Park Commission had specified a location commanding an "undisputed domination over a large area, together with a certain dignified isolation from competing structures." The site was raised to give it a more dominant position.

The Lincoln Memorial was designed by Henry Bacon in a classical Greek temple manner. It is a wonderful marriage of a classical building to its site and is especially impressive when viewed at night. The enormous seated statue of Abraham Lincoln inside was designed by Daniel Chester French, who spent thirteen years sculpting it. It is so arresting and so impressive that visitors often stand transfixed in awe, almost as if expecting Lincoln to speak to them. In fact, he does, since the texts of his Gettysburg and Second Inaugural Addresses are etched into the nearby walls.

The cultural atmosphere of Washington in 1835 improved remarkably. The national museum – the Smithsonian Institution – had its beginning at that time.

Actually, it started in the mind of its founder well before that. James Smithson was born in France in 1765, but because he was the illegitimate son of Hugh Smithson, the first Duke of Northumberland, he was forced to live under the name of James Lewis Macie for the first fifty years of his life. By the time the crown finally allowed him to take his real name, he had become a noted scientist and very wealthy.

He never married and he never visited America. Yet, in his will, he stated if his nephew died without an heir (which he did) his entire estate should go "to the United States of America, to found at Washington under the name of the Smithsonian Institution, an establishment for the increase and diffusion of knowledge among men." Then, he added, "My name shall live in the memory of man when the titles of the Northumberlands and Percys are extinct and forgotten."

Smithson's estate amounted to $550,000, a princely sum in 1835. At first the Smithsonian Institution conducted scientific research and published the findings, but it just kept growing.

Under Smithson's broad caveat, almost anything was possible. A distinguished scientist, Joseph Henry, was named the Smithsonian's first secretary and his principles still guide the museum. "The great object is to facilitate... the promotion of science... the fostering of original research, and enlarging the bounds of human thought." He believed that no subject should be excluded.

Accordingly, one of his first acts was to put Samuel Morse's new telegraphs to use. In 1847, Henry proposed "to organize a system of observation which will extend as far as possible over the North American continent... The extended lines of the telegraph will furnish a ready means of warning the more northern and eastern observers (weather in the eastern United States usually moves from the west or southwest) to be on the watch from the first appearance of an advancing storm." This was the forerunner of the

National Weather Service.

In 1847 the first Smithsonian building was designed by architect James Renwick, Jr. With its crenelated towers and red sandstone walls, it would look more at home on the banks of the Thames in England than on the Mall in Washington. It's still known as the "Castle."

It originally housed a science museum, lecture hall, research laboratories and living quarters for secretary Henry and his family.

The Institution outgrew its walls long ago. The original building is used now for administrative offices, except for a small room just off the entrance, which contains James Smithson's tomb. He would undoubtedly be proud to see what his original gift has produced.

Today, the Smithsonian complex is the largest museum in the world, composed of twelve museums and the zoo in Washington, as well as the Cooper-Hewitt Museum in New York. Most folks know it as "the nation's attic" because it houses over 100 million artifacts of historic or scientific interest.

The Smithsonian outgrew its first building by 1876. A new one was precipitated by the Philadelphia Centennial of the same year. At the end of the six-month World's Fair, exhibitors simply crated the contents of their exhibits and shipped them to Washington. There were forty-five freight cars in all and nowhere to put them.

Congress appropriated $250,000 for a new National Museum that contains an enormous skylit rotunda with a fountain in its center. The soaring walls were used originally to hang flags and banners and the exterior is reminiscent of the original "Castle" next door. The building has a certain sense of friendliness and gaiety. It's almost as if this building continues the spirit of the Philadelphia Centennial celebrations, and in fact, it does. The contents of the museum continue to exhibit the contents of those forty-five freight cars of exhibitry.

The Smithsonian's secretary in 1876 was Spencer Fullerton Baird, a scientist himself. He amassed a wonderful collection of artifacts and specimens from various governmental expeditions. Under his leadership, the Smithsonian became a center of biological and geological research. He encouraged expeditions and pleaded that the finding be sent to the Smithsonian. His daughter wrote, "No bride ever devoted more thought and attention to her trousseau than did my father to fitting out each of these explorers."

The galleries are filled with popular books of the 1870s, including Uncle Tom's Cabin and cookbooks, the telegraph invented by Samuel F.B. Morse (which he first demonstrated in Washington in 1844), carriages, lace, furniture, silverware, a printing press, an ice cream maker, military uniforms and chinaware. The Virginia exhibit in Philadelphia even included a small leather purse once carried by Pocahontas – and that's there too.

Even though the Smithsonian takes great care in looking after its collections and buildings, the National Museum, now called the Arts and Industries Building, needed renovation by the mid-twentieth century. The Smithsonian gave it a thorough overhaul, just in time for a grand rededication in 1976, in celebration of the Bicentennial. Now it's looking better than ever!

Before long it was apparent that even two buildings were not enough to house all the collections of the Smithsonian. Scientists on expeditions needed more room to display their artifacts. Dinosaur bones, precious minerals, unusual rocks, stuffed animals, were all looking for a place to stay. So, in 1910 the "new" National Museum was built. It's now referred to as the National Museum of Natural History and is one of the most popular in the entire collection of museums.

On entering the museum it's hard to miss the enormous, eight-ton, thirteen-foot tall bull elephant killed in Africa in 1955. Then it's on to fossil exhibits, some that appeared in the ocean as much as 600 million years ago. There's a dinosaur gallery that features sloths, saber-toothed cats and a huge flying reptile. Other galleries contain exhibits on the cultures of Asia, Africa, the Eskimos and the American Indians.

One of the most popular rooms in the Natural History Museum, however, is the "Life in the Sea" room, where aquariums duplicate actual marine environments in existence in a tropical Caribbean reef and along the rocky coast of Maine. In the former, it's possible to see tropical fish, crabs, corals and their support systems almost as if you were there diving in the waters of the Caribbean.

The Maine Coast environment shows lobsters and crab walking among clams, scallops, mussels, and kelp. It's all so realistic that there are even waves splashing against the coral or rock outcroppings and the tide rises and falls at the rate of a foot twice a day.

And then there's the mineral and gem collection.

Scores of visitors wend their way around the Mineral Gallery on their way to the Hall of Gems. Along the way they'll learn about the California gold rush. Once inside the Hall of Gems, most people head straight for the fabulous Hope diamond, a 45.5-carat deep blue diamond, which has a fascinating history.

In 1668, a fabulous, large "French blue" diamond was taken from India to France to be added to the crown jewels of King Louis XIV. It was stolen in 1792 and never recovered. It's thought the Hope, purchased in 1830 by Henry Thomas Hope of England, may have been cut from the French crown jewel.

Legend says a curse hangs over the Hope diamond and who knows? Evalyn McLean, whose husband's family owned the Washington Post, purchased the diamond in the early 1900s. Shortly thereafter their son died, the McLeans separated and Mr. McLean was declared insane. In 1949 the Hope diamond was obtained by The New York jeweler Harry Winston, who gave it to the Smithsonian in 1959.

The Hope diamond is not alone in the Hall of Gems. The room rivals the Crown Jewel room in the Tower of London for brilliance. There's a 127-carat Portuguese diamond, a 138-7 carat ruby, a 423-carat sapphire and a 37.8-carat deep green emerald. There's also a 31-carat heart-shaped blue diamond, once owned by French Empress Eugenie and the 330-carat Star of Asia, one of the world's largest cabochon-cut sapphires.

The Freer Gallery of Art, on the other side of the original "Castle" from the Arts and Industries building, was the gift of one man. Charles Lang Freer was born in New York in 1854. He left school at 14, worked briefly in a cement factory and for a railroad and eventually moved to Detroit and founded the Peninsular Car Works, the first factory to manufacture railroad cars in the United States. The Railway Age was just getting under way. Freer's cars were solid and well-designed and he prospered.

In 1899, Freer sold his company for several million dollars and retired to enjoy his hobby of collecting art. He traveled the world and became especially interested in the work of James McNeill Whistler. Although Whistler lived in London, he was an American. One day Freer decided to visit the artist he admired so much and thus began an unusual but fulfilling friendship–unusual because there was over twenty years difference in the men's ages and fulfilling because Freer continued to learn and grow in his study of art. Whistler

taught Freer the beauty of Oriental art.

Freer was a fastidious dandy, of whom it was said, "He was aghast at crude manners... and offended at anything but the most chivalrous conduct toward women... Some of the Detroit industrialists complained that 'Charley Freer was no good on a picnic,' preferring to talk of the tariff on Italian paintings rather than the price of steel."

In 1903 Freer offered to give his now extensive art collection to the nation. Up to that time the art collection of the Smithsonian consisted mainly of Indian art and historical paintings with a few miscellaneous exceptions. Freer's collection now amounted to over two thousand objects. Along with this gift he would provide a building to house the collection in. Freer worked closely with the architect Charles Platt to be sure it would fit his needs.

The museum opened in 1921. In addition to the extensive Whistler collection, which includes 128 paintings (but not "Whistler's Mother", which is in the Louvre), 163 works in pencil, ink and pastel and 944 prints, there's a Chinese bronze collection, Chinese porcelains and ceramics and a collection of Islamic paintings. But the pride of the museum is the remarkable Peacock Room.

A Liverpool shipbuilder, Frederick Leyland, was Whistler's first patron. He designed a dining room to display his extensive collection of blue and white Oriental porcelain and he asked Whistler to compose a painting to be hung over the mantlepiece. His painting, "Rose and Silver; The Princess From the Land of Porcelain" was an exquisite and delicate complement to the Chinese porcelain.

Unfortunately, the room in which it was all displayed was decorated in red and, to Whistler's mind, clashed with his painting. So Leyland gave him permission to make a few adjustments. Whistler made the changes while Leyland was away for several months and when he came back, Leyland could scarcely believe his eyes.

The valuable antique red Spanish leather walls had been painted over with turquoise and gold peacocks and the walnut shelves and fireplace and irons had been gilded. Whistler called the room "Harmony in Blue and Gold."

Whistler said, "Pictures have been painted often enough with consideration of the room in which they hang; in this case I have painted a room to harmonize with my picture."

Leyland was horrified and paid Whistler only half the price he asked and he paid in pounds rather than guineas. Out of spite, Whistler changed one of the paintings decorating the room to depict a wealthy peacock clutching a pile of silver coins in his claw, while a poor peacock disdains the silver.

Leyland later grew to love the room and when he died it was exactly as Whistler left it. The room was sold at auction in 1892. It wasn't until 1904 that Freer was finally able to purchase it. He felt $30,000 was a fair price for such a treasure. He added a new wing to his Detroit house to show off his purchase. It now occupies the position of honor in the Freer Gallery and should not be missed.

The National Gallery of Art was added to the Smithsonian in 1941. The collection encompasses the history of Western art from the twelfth century to the present. This is one of the finest repositories of Western art in America, thanks to the generosity of Andrew W. Mellon. The former secretary of the treasury decided to collect art for the specific purpose of forming the nucleus of a national art gallery.

Such renowned art dealers as Knoedler and Duveen Brothers vied for the privilege of selling Mellon their finest works. In fact, Duveen even rented an apartment directly below Mellon's in Washington where he displayed potential purchases for Mellon to view at his leisure.

After the Russian Revolution, the Hermitage was willing to sell some of its masterpieces. Mellon bought twenty-one of the finest – mostly old masters, including Botticelli, Raphael, Titian, Rembrandt, Van Dyck and Frans Hals.

By the time Mellon went to London as Ambassador in 1932, he had amassed a truly remarkable collection. With his death in 1937, the government made his gift official by granting a charter to the National Gallery of Art.

The building to house this magnificent collection was designed by John Russell Pope. It's a grandiose and sumptuous building, with marble halls, travertine fountains and bronze figurines.

The gallery's first curator, John Walker said, "The building was intended to satisfy an often unrecognized desire on the part of the public. In this country there is a lack of the magnificent churches, public buildings and palaces of Europe; Americans living for the most part in apartments and small houses feel the need for buildings more sumptuous, more spacious and less utilitarian than their everyday surroundings."

Since the gallery opened in 1941, other impressive collections and paintings have been added to Mellon's original, including a donation of the only Leonardo da Vinci outside Europe.

To house this expanding collection of art, a new building was opened in 1978. Where the classic lines of the West Building were gentle and pure, the new building's by I.M. Pei and Associates, are bold and bright. The spaces are filled with light from glass walls and ceiling. As is appropriate, the new wing houses primarily the work of modern painters.

And yet, there still wasn't enough room in the Smithsonian. In 1964, the National Museum of American History, then called the Museum of History and Technology, was opened. This museum, designed by McKim Mead and White, is so vast that it might be considered several museums all wrapped into one. But its variety leaves little room for boredom.

It's here that the original Star Spangled Banner hangs, protected now from the harmful effects of light and air. There are automobiles, clocks and timepieces, coins, medals, money, firearms, a large exhibit on the development of American newspapers, textiles, political memorabilia and special exhibits. One called "After the Revolution: Everyday Life in America 1780-1800" recreates the actual homes of American patriots and allows visitors to walk into their parlors to see how they lived.

Without question, however, the most popular exhibit in the National Museum of American History is the First Ladies Hall. Here, one can step back in time and visualize the First Ladies on their inauguration days. The first inaugural gown in the collection dates from 1829 and most of the gowns worn by the First Ladies did actually belong to them.

All the Ladies are grouped in White House settings made to resemble the White House of their own day. Some are in the music room, some in the Blue Room and some in the Red Room. The Red Room is the final setting, showing it as it looked after being redecorated in 1962 by Jacqueline Kennedy in the 1810-1830s style. The First Ladies from Kennedy to Reagan are resplendent here in their inaugural gowns.

In 1974 the Hirshhorn Museum and Sculpture Garden were added to the collection of Smithsonian Institution buildings. Joseph Hirshhorn was an immigrant from Latvia, who came to the United States at the age of six. His widowed mother worked in a purse factory in Brooklyn to support herself and her ten children. Hirschhorn left school at age fourteen and was a wiz on Wall Street by the time he was seventeen.

He loved art from the time of his childhood. At first, he tacked pictures from colorful calendars on his walls, but he soon expanded to historical etchings and finally to paintings. His specialty was modern art. He would just as soon buy a painting that appealed to him by an unknown artist, as buy from a recognized name.

By the time Hirschhorn reached the age of 30 he was a millionaire, with enough wisdom to sell his stocks prior to the famous crash of 1929. Later, he mined hundreds of millions of tons of uranium in Canada.

During his entire lifetime Hirshhorn continued to collect. By the 1960s his unique collection was being eagerly sought by various nations. But Hirschhorn never forget his immigrant roots and the opportunity afforded him by the United States. He wanted his collection to become part of the national treasury. The building that houses this magnificent collection sits on the Mall.

To view the Hirschhorn Museum collection is like taking a tour of modern art. It is arranged relatively chronologically so that the progress of American art literally unfolds before the onlooker's eyes. The paintings include works by Thomas Eakins, John Singer Sargent and Georgia O'Keefe. The sculptures include such great artists as Rodin and Henry Moore. This is where the monumental "The Burghers of Calais" by Rodin is housed.

From the uniqueness of modern art to the uniqueness of the latest museum in the Smithsonian collection is no great jump. The National Air and Space Museum opened in 1976, just in time for the Bicentennial. This is the most popular museum in the entire Smithsonian complex and, in fact, in the world, welcoming some ten million people annually. What makes this museum so popular? Perhaps it's partly the building itself. It's basically a glass-enclosed box that somehow extends the walls of the museum outward to include the Mall as well.

Inside, there are exhibits to fascinate young and old alike. There are objects as old as a seventeenth-century Chinese sundial and as new as the spacecraft. There are historic airplanes hanging from the beams. These include the Wright Brothers' plane and Charles Lindbergh's *Spirit of St. Louis*. There's Chuck Yeager's plane, the first one to break the sound barrier, as well as John Glenn's *Friendship 7*, the first U.S. spacecraft to orbit the earth.

A visit to the National Air and Space Museum can easily take the better part of a day, especially since no one wants to miss the exhilarating movies shown on an extra large screen. This is as much a museum to feel and experience in as it is to see. You can walk through an actual Skylab, touch a lunar rock and feel the sensation of being on the flight deck of an aircraft carrier as planes land and take off.

All these various museums are only part of the Smithsonian experience. There's no doubt about it, if James Smithson can see today's result of his initial legacy, he's smiling a big Cheshire grin up there in heaven.

After President Lincoln's assassination, the capital felt that nothing so terrible would ever happen again. Special precautions were taken to protect the President and soon the incident dimmed in memory. Throughout the 1870s, residents enjoyed the new Smithsonian Museum, they promenaded in the Mall Downing had designed for them and, in general, enjoyed themselves.

Government was growing too. The Department of Agriculture, which ten years earlier had been the property of one patriotic gentleman who distributed free seed and plants, was now large enough to build its own building on the Mall.

There had been a State, War and Navy Building since 1800 but they had outgrown their walls. It was natural, then, in 1871 to build a new one. The building was completed in 1887. Frank Carpenter wrote, "(It) is said to be the largest granite structure in the world. It is so built that it will almost outlast the ages. As I stand here on this marble pavement and think of the lives that will be eaten up in this building, and of the enterprise shriveled into inertia, it makes me shudder." We know this magnificent pile of columns and gingerbread today as the Old Executive Office Building.

When President Garfield was elected in 1880, he was considered a rather nondescript man. He was an ex-general and an ex-Congressman, who found himself thrust into the leadership of a country that continued to bear the scars of a Civil War; a country that had not resolved the conflict between negroes and whites and that had a high unemployment rate. But, to start his presidency on a high note, he held his inaugural ball in the newly completed National Museum (now the Arts and Industries Building).

His Presidency was destined to be short-lived, however, for he was shot on July 2, 1881. Jane Gemmill, a resident of Washington, recorded the atmosphere:

"July 4, 1881. What a remarkable country this

is, and how rapidly events follow each other, keeping one in a perpetual state of excitement!... Yesterday the city was radiant with inaugural festivities, today it is dark, gloomy, uncertain! The President has been stricken down by the hand of an assassin and no one can foretell the result.

"I stood on Saturday morning last on the same spot where I was standing the 4th day of March, as the newly made President rose in his carriage, bowed to the cheering multitude, and was swirled in through the south gate leading to the Executive Mansion...

"(On Saturday) I stopped for a few moments at the White House gate, about sunset, to learn the latest tidings from the sick chamber. Groups were standing all along the square waiting for the same purpose. High and low were there, and each seemed equally interested.

"September. If the contrast between the journey of the President on March 4th and July 2nd was very great, I think the early morning ride of yesterday greater still. Lifted from his couch by tender and loving hands, laid upon a mattress in an express wagon, and driven between daybreak and sunrise... the patient slowly, slowly dying and longing, longing for the sight of the sea. The President has longed so much to go to the seashore that his physicians decided to gratify him, and the preparations for the journey were begun some days ago...

"In order to avoid driving over rough cobblestones to the car, the railroad company kindly ordered a branch track laid up to the very edge of the concrete pavement on Pennsylvania Avenue.

"September 23. Pennsylvania Avenue is clothed today in the habiliments of mourning. With muffled drums, measured steps, and bowed heads, the people have paid the last sad honor to James A. Garfield."

And yet, life went on. The National Theater, destroyed by fire, was rebuilt again in 1886. Frank Carp dutifully reported that "All fashionable Washington" was at the opening. "The beaux appeared in their claw-hammer coats, the belles were attired in evening dress... This new theater is the talk of the town, the verdict being that it is one of the coziest, prettiest, and best appointed houses in the country."

John Philip Sousa had become conductor of the U.S. Marine Band in 1880 and he brought a new level of entertainment to band music. Sousa was the son of a band member and started playing with the band in 1868, when he was thirteen. He stayed for seven years and then left to play music elsewhere. In 1880 he returned to lead the Marine Band. This time he stayed for twelve years. While there, he composed such national favorites as "The Stars and Stripes Forever," and "Semper Fidelis." In his own autobiography he wrote, "The Commandant had impressed upon me the necessity of a complete reorganization of the band. The men were dissatisfied with the present state of affairs, and to use the Commandant's words, 'The band gives me more trouble than the rest of the corp put together.'

"By the end of the first year the band was reduced to thirty-three men and even the Commandant was a little alarmed; but I gradually gathered about me an ambitious and healthy lot of young players, and the public performances of the band began to attract very favorable attention from Washingtonians and visitors to the National Capital.

"From a motley mob of nurses and baby carriages and some hangers-on, the audiences at the White House Grounds concerts grew into the thousands and the Saturday afternoon concerts at the Barracks were splendidly attended and Wednesday concerts at the Capitol drew large audiences, although we suffered from the noise of carriages passing."

In the White House not much happened to relieve virtual boredom, except for a 9-day celebration attending President Grover Cleveland's wedding in the White House in 1893 – the first and only Presidential marriage. Not much, that is, until Teddy Roosevelt burst on the scene in 1901.

Roosevelt came to Washington in 1890 to serve as a member of the new Civil Service Commission. President Harrison said of him, "The only trouble I ever had managing him was that he wanted to put an end to all the evil in the world between sunrise and sunset."

Roosevelt had worked his way up to Assistant Secretary of the Navy when the Spanish-American War was upon the nation. He resigned from the Navy to lead his Rough Riders in battle against the Spanish.

John Hay, American minister to London, said of the war. "It had been a splendid little war, begun with the highest motives, carried on with magnificent intelligence and spirit, favored by that future which loves the brave."

Back from the war, Roosevelt was elected President in 1901. He and his family filled the White House with delicious nonsense. It was said, "In the White House his life as a father, as a husband, as a citizen, as a politician, was most interesting, but almost primitive in its simplicity. Few forms were observed... He talked state secrets in a loud voice to statesmen in the presidential workroom, so that reporters could hear. He went on long walks through the parks in the environ of Washington taking fat military officers with him, who panted along a step of two behind. He tolerated no sacred cows."

One of those outings has been charmingly and humorously preserved by the French minister Jusserand, who sent the following account back to France, "President Roosevelt invited me to take a promenade with him this afternoon at three. I arrived at the White House punctually, in afternoon dress and silk hat, as if to stroll in the Tuileries... To my surprise, the President soon joined me in a tramping suit, with knickerbockers and thick boots... On reaching the country, the President went pell-mell over the fields... At last we came to the bank of a stream rather too wide and deep to be forded... But judge of my horror when I saw the President unbutton his clothes and heard him say 'We had better strip, so as not to wet our things in the Creek.' Then I, too, for the honor of France removed my apparel, everything except my lavender kid gloves. The President cast an inquiring look at these as if they, too, must come off, but I quickly forestalled any remark by saying, 'With your permission, Mr. President, I will keep these on; otherwise it would be embarrassing if we should meet ladies.' And so we jumped in the water and swam across."

Roosevelt's Presidency was followed by the austere and isolated Presidency of Woodrow Wilson and then the relaxed and careless Presidency of Warren Harding. The Teapot Dome and Elk Hills scandals set Washington on its ear in the 1920s.

By the 1930s it was clear the nation was in economic distress and the full force of this distress was brought to Washington by several hunger marches. Unemployed veterans arrived in June of 1932 to set up crude camps in Washington near the White House. They demanded payment of a war bonus. They were eventually routed but not until Federal troops were called to drive them out.

In 1933 Franklin Delano Roosevelt was elected to the Presidency. He brought a new vigor and sense of hope. For the first time, Roosevelt encouraged an outreach to foreign nations that was the forerunner of a planned foreign policy.

Meanwhile, determined to defeat the depression and create a better social and economic climate, he had instituted his "New Deal." He conducted "fireside chats," where he candidly and forthrightly told the public, by radio, what he hoped to accomplish. He was a popular president. Roosevelt is the only President elected to office three times. His third inaugural parade in 1941 was witnessed by at least a million people.

And then he was dead. Shortly after his third inauguration Roosevelt died of a cerebral hemorrhage. He had led the United States through the horror of Hitler in the Second World War and then had died.

He was followed by Harry Truman, who had an interesting problem in the White House himself. Shortly after taking office, the Trumans had a rather harrowing experience.

One day Mrs. Truman was walking through the Blue Room when she noticed the chandelier wavering at an odd tilt. Then Margaret Truman saw that one leg of her piano was sinking into the floor. Engineers gave the house a thorough analysis and realized that virtually all the timbers were splitting or rotting under the stress of age and new heating, ventilating and plumbing systems. Almost before they'd unpacked their bags, the Trumans were packed up again and moved across the street to Blair House. It took almost four years before they were allowed to move back in. In the meantime, the White House got a new concrete foundation, steel framework throughout and fireproofing.

The golden era of Washington arrived in 1960 with the election of John Fitzgerald Kennedy. The mystique – the charisma – of both John F. and Jacqueline Kennedy captured the hearts of America, perhaps at a time when America needed something to believe in most. America was certainly still reeling from the effects of the Second World War.

The Kennedys took Washington by storm. This was not the normal aloof Presidency. Kennedy had made it clear in the beginning that he felt the President of the United States should himself be a symbol of freedom. To him, this meant that he should appear as a free man among free men and not as one constantly surrounded by bodyguards. This gave the Secret Service high blood pressure.

Kennedy had been raised in Massachusetts. His father had been Ambassador to the Court of St. James in London under Roosevelt, and Kennedy himself had been elected twice to Congress and twice to the Senate. He was not a stranger to politics or to Washington. Even

Jacqueline had worked in the capital for a while.

Kennedy was a U.S. Senator when he married Jacqueline Bouvier. She was charming and delightful; beautiful and talented. He was brilliant and powerful; handsome and very wealthy. The gossip columnists reported every move the Kennedys made and the public loved it.

From a social history perspective, it's perhaps Jacqueline who left the greatest impact. Over the years, many art objects, decorations and furniture that had once graced the White House had been lost, sold or thrown away. It now reflected no distinctive American style, but represented a hodge podge of leftovers that had appealed to one Presidential family or another.

And then Jacqueline Kennedy arrived on the scene. Young, enthusiastic and interested in history and historic preservation, she assumed the task of restoring the White House state rooms to their early nineteenth-century appearance. She appointed a committee to research the appearance of each room originally and to find missing objects. Thanks to her efforts, the White House is now a museum devoted to the finest in American furnishings, as well as the home of the First Family.

As to John Kennedy, the moving words of his inaugural address rang in America's ears: "And so, my fellow Americans, ask not what your country can do for you; ask what you can do for your country.

"All this will not be finished in the first one hundred days. Nor will it be finished in the first one thousand days, nor in the life of this Administration, nor even perhaps in our lifetime on this planet. But let us begin."

Later, he observed: "Our problems are manmade – therefore they can be solved by man... For, in the final analysis, our most basic common link is that we all inhabit this small planet. We all breathe the same air. We all cherish our children's future. And we are all mortal."

But who was to know that on a tragic day in November 1963, merely 1000 days after he was elected President, President Kennedy's life would be snuffed out. But there, in Dallas, Lee Harvey Oswald aimed a rifle with deadly accuracy at President Kennedy's head and killed him. America mourned and the world mourned. The magic, the brilliance and the mystery all seemed hollow now.

World opinion reflected the loss. Clinton Rossiter, a political scientist, said, "As a President, he will, alas, be remembered as one to whom greatness... was denied" because death "claimed him long before his hour..."

Le Figaro in Paris commented, "What remains as the loss... is a certain feeling of possibilities, of an elan, and – why not say it? – of an impression of beauty. These are not political qualities, but surely they are enduring legendary and mythological qualities."

It's hard to forget the words of Jacqueline Kennedy, who poignantly and tragically said in a Look magazine article on the first anniversary of Kennedy's death, "On so many days – his birthday, an anniversary, watching his children run to the sea – I have thought, 'But this day last year was his last to see that.' He was so full of love and life on those days. He seems so vulnerable now, when you think that each one was a last time...

"Now I think that I should have known that he was magic all along. I did know it – but I should have guessed it could not last. I should have known that it was asking too much to dream that I might have grown old with him and see our children grow up together.

"So now he is a legend when he would have preferred to be a man..."

The nation grieved and hurt dreadfully, but life in Washington did go on – not with the same radiance – but it did go on. The Kennedy years were hard acts to follow and who would have known the undercurrent of unrest that would at first bubble up and then erupted into the violent clash of opinions relating to equality for blacks and to the Vietnam War.

Now Washington saw plenty! The Civil Rights movement had exploded into race riots in a black district of Los Angeles in 1965. The Watts riots left 34 dead and 1,032 injured. The next year it was Cleveland's turn and then Detroit and Newark. Demonstrations were held on the once-placid lawn of the Mall as early as the 1963 "March on Washington." In 1968, Washington had its own full-fledged riots. Stores were looted two blocks from the White House.

Martin Luther King had planned a "Poor People's Campaign." There would be a march on Washington which would culminate in the erection of a "Resurrection City." This was to be a tangible and visible plea for help for the poor. King's untimely assassination in 1968 left his associate Ralph D. Abernathy to lead the campaign, which he did. A tent city was erected as planned on the Mall, but that was temporary.

And then, at the end of 1968, Richard M. Nixon was elected. He was the ultimate politician. He had weathered storms over the years. First there was the Alger Hiss trial, then his election defeats (notably against John F. Kennedy), but he was a survivor.

Yet Nixon was about to precipitate one of the nation's greatest scandals. On June 17, 1972 the Democratic headquarters in the fancy Watergate apartment complex in Washington was broken into. Little public attention was paid to the robbery at the time. But after the election in November, the plot got thicker and thicker. It was soon apparent that Nixon's closest advisors – and even Nixon himself – had been involved in either planning the break-in or in participating in a cover-up.

But even as late as November 11, 1973, Nixon was loudly proclaiming, "I made my mistakes, but in all my years of public life I have never profited from public service. I have earned every cent... I welcome this kind of examination because people have got to know whether or not their President is a crook. Well, I'm not a crook."

But was he? On August 9, 1974, Richard Nixon resigned under tremendous pressure to do so. He was the first president in the history of the United States to do so. Had he not, he probably would have been impeached.

Perhaps the United States is at its best, however, in the face of adversity. Somehow, it just marches on. Troubles are put behind and the look is to the future.

History is often better viewed from a distance rather than up close. It's the long perspective that helps us understand what we may have been too close to grasp at the time.

And that's the glory of Washington. Washington rather envelops the government of the United States. It's a repository of power and the conscience of the nation. No matter what the social, economic or politican issue, it receives its forum in Washington.

Yes, Ninian Beall would be surprised to see what the government of the United States has done with the land that was given him by the crown all those years ago, but he'd be even more surprised to see what that government has become. For all its faults, its strengths are greater. Somehow, when the fog has cleared, the government still goes on – perhaps even stronger for the adversity it's endured.

The Washington Monument (previous page), completed in 1884 is the tallest masonry obelisk in the world and commemorates the nation's first president. Encircled by fifty flags, each one representing a state, this simple yet imposing pillar draws over a million visitors a year. A "watermark," visible in the marble nearly halfway up the monument, was the unfortunate consequence of the lengthy pause in construction between 1855 and 1876. Left: the United States Capitol, probably the best loved and most revered building in America, and (overleaf) the South Portico of the White House. The once-controversial second-floor balcony was designed by President Truman in 1948. Most of the rooms behind these windows are open to the public during guided tours of this, the official residence of the President and the country's most famous mansion.

Facing page: (top) the marble exterior of the Lincoln Memorial, which overlooks the Reflecting Pool, and (bottom) the John F. Kennedy Center for the Performing Arts, which serves as a memorial for one of America's most intellectual Presidents. The Marine Corps War Memorial (above) salutes marines killed in battle. Overleaf: red brick residential Washington beside the great white buildings of government.

A cloudless winter's evening forms a serene
backdrop for the classical lines of the Jefferson
Memorial. Thomas Jefferson, the third President of
the United States, was a a multi-talented man who
not only drafted the Declaration of Independence
but also won recognition in roles as varied as those
of inventor, architect, philosopher and botanist. The
memorial, which was dedicated by President
Franklin D. Roosevelt in 1943, has as its centerpiece
a nineteen-foot-high bronze of Jefferson. The walls
surrounding him bear excerpts from the two
documents for which this eighteenth-century
Renaissance man most wanted to be remembered –
the Declaration of Independence and the Virginia
Statute for Religious Freedom.

Although the statues that form the centerpieces of the Lincoln (above) and Jefferson (top) memorials are huge when seen close to, when viewed from a distance at night they appear to be on a more human scale. The statue of Abraham Lincoln in particular is lit to superb effect; the President seems to be watching and waiting, his gaze directed down to the Washington Monument (facing page), towards Capitol Hill and the great white dome of the Capitol (overleaf), his steady expression seemingly one of strict determination that the country's leaders should not fail the nation he served so well.

Above left: the distinctive arches of Daniel Burnham's Beaux Arts Union Station, now a shopping mall, and (left) the National Museum of American History and Technology on the Mall (above and overleaf). For eighty years this "Grand Avenue," designed as the national mall by Washington's planner Pierre L'Enfant, was subject to considerable neglect due to lack of money. Some of the land was so marshy that the Washington Monument could not be built in its intended position for fear it would topple. It was only at the turn of the century that the government found the funds to drain the land and cultivate the green lawns, trees and colorful flowerbeds of today.

These pages and overleaf: the National Air and Space Museum, an imaginatively designed building that allows for aircraft to be displayed as if in flight. Some of the most famous airplanes in history are here, such as the Spirit of St Louis – Charles Lindbergh's choice for the first solo flight across the Atlantic – and the Wright Brothers' craft in which Orville Wright made the first manned flight.

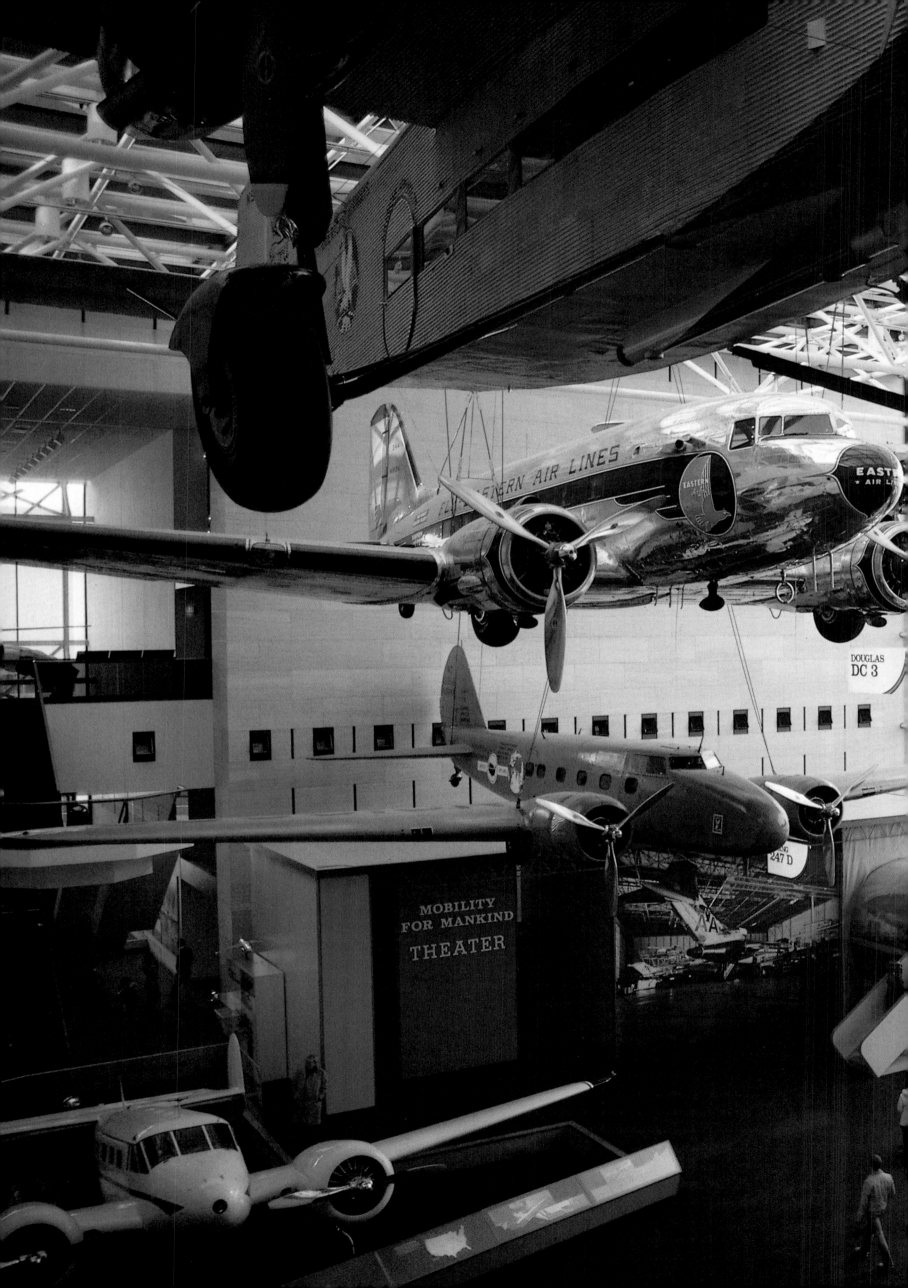

IN MEMORIAM

CREW OF SPACE SHUTTLE MISSION 51-L *CHALLENGER*, JANUARY 28, 1986

The crew of *Challenger* was lost as a result of an in-flight explosion, shortly after the launch of the Space Shuttle.

Ellison S. Onizuka, mission specialist. Born June 24, 1946, Kealakekua, Kona, Hawaii. He became a NASA astronaut in 1978.

S. Christa Corrigan McAuliffe, teacher. Born September 2, 1948, Boston, Massachusetts. She was selected as the primary candidate for the Teacher in Space project in July 1985.

Gregory B. Jarvis, payload specialist. Born August 24, 1944, Detroit, Michigan. He was selected as a payload specialist from Hughes Aircraft Corp. in 1984.

Judith A. Resnik, mission specialist. Born April 15, 1949, Akron, Ohio. She became a NASA astronaut in 1978.

Michael J. Smith, pilot. Born April 30, 1945, Beaufort, North Carolina. He became a NASA astronaut in 1980.

Francis R. (Dick) Scobee, spacecraft commander. Born May 19, 1939, Cle Elum, Washington. He became a NASA astronaut in 1978.

Ronald E. McNair, mission specialist. Born October 21, 1950, Lake City, South Carolina. He became a NASA astronaut in 1978.

Left: a scale model of the Challenger Space Shuttle and a memorial plaque draped in black silk in the National Air and Space Museum (above). As a horrified TV audience looked on, the crew of seven was killed when the shuttle exploded shortly after take-off on January 28, 1986. As part of its Albert Einstein Spacearium the museum also displays the Skylab Oribital Workshop, which visitors are invited to explore, and a piece of moon rock that they are allowed to touch. In addition, special films on flight are projected onto a five-story movie screen in the museum theater; throughout the twenty-three galleries imaginative use is made of the latest audio-visual technology.

Above: the famous African bush elephant, the largest known specimen ever displayed, in the National Museum of Natural History (these pages), part of the Smithsonian Institution. This museum boasts more than sixty million objects in its research collections, its exhibits ranging from dinosaurs to unicorn beetles. Overleaf: the "Castle," as the first home of the Smithsonian Institution has been dubbed .

These pages: displays in the Arts and Industries Building, the second-oldest Smithsonian building on the Mall. This was used for President James Garfield's inaugural ball in 1881 and today houses "1876: A Centennial Exhibition," one of the most extensive collections of American Victoriana ever presented in an original setting. The great exhibit halls have been restored to their original appearance, recalling the atmosphere of the late nineteenth century, and they house, among a host of smaller items, working steam engines, a gleaming Baldwin locomotive (right) of 1876 and a fifty-one-foot model of the Naval sloop of war, Antietam.

Left: the majestic marbled Rotunda that greets visitors to the National Gallery of Art (above left). Here is to be found one of the world's finest collections of paintings; the gallery can boast the only Leonado da Vinci outside Europe and the most comprehensive survey of Italian art in the western hemisphere. All of the works of art owned by the gallery have been given by private citizens or purchased with their donated funds. The gallery's West Building was the gift of the former Secretary of the Treasury, Andrew Mellon, in 1937 and the East Building (overleaf), designed by I.M. Pei and opened in 1978, was financed by Paul Mellon, the late Ailsa Mellon Bruce and the Andrew W. Mellon Foundation. Above: part of the fascinating Sculpture Garden of the Hirshhorn Museum, which houses a collection of mainly modern American art.

Right: the Main Reading Room of the Library of Congress (overleaf). The Library is thought to be the largest single repository of knowledge anywhere in the world. It is certainly one of the most palatial, the ornamental detail, both within the building and on its exterior, being strikingly lavish. Anyone over eighteen can use the library, but priority is given to Congressmen and women and their aides. There are eighty-six million items held here – among the most surprising perhaps being five Stradivarius violins and 1,500 flutes. Four hundred items are added every hour. The library was begun in 1800 as a one-room reference collection for Congress. When this was burned in 1814 by the British, Thomas Jefferson sold his private library to the government to replace it. Containing 6,500 items it was the finest in the country at that time. Today, in memory of that gesture, there is a reading room in the library named in honor of the third President.

Above: the Capitol's Statuary Hall, which, since 1864, has been a showcase for statues of America's great men and women. Each state is allowed two sculptures of persons felt to have been influential in its history, such as Brigham Young in the case of Utah and Robert E. Lee in that of Virginia. Left and overleaf: the Capitol Building. When L'Enfant planned the city in 1790 he considered Jenkins Hill – now known as Capitol Hill, or simply, to Washingtonians, "the Hill" – to be "a pedestal waiting for a monument." The monument he had in mind was the Capitol of the new republic, fittingly placed upon the highest ground in the area. Ironically, the bronze Statue of Freedom that tops the Capitol's dome was cast by slave labor. Above left: the dome's interior, as grand as its exterior.

Although it was once dubbed "Jefferson's muffin" for its low, circular shape and "a cage for Jefferson's statue" in reference to its encircling fifty-four columns, the Jefferson Memorial (these pages and overleaf) is one of Washington's most popular attractions. Situated in the Tidal Basin, the memorial is dominated by Rudolph Evans' statue of Jefferson, who is depicted addressing the Declaration of Independence committee. Surrrounding the memorial and the Tidal Basin are the cherry trees that the city of Tokyo presented to the city of Washington in 1912. These are much loved by the city's residents; during the Forties some of them had to be moved for the memorial to be built, and indignant tree-lovers protested by chaining themselves to the chosen trees and later occupying the holes left by the uprooted ones. Such conflict is forgotten today; the temple-like structure appears all the more serene for its surrounding trees, especially in spring, when their blossom complements the marble of the memorial.

WE HOLD THESE TRUTHS TO BE SELF-
EVIDENT, THAT ALL MEN ARE CREATED
EQUAL, THAT THEY ARE ENDOWED BY THEIR
CREATOR WITH CERTAIN INALIENABLE
RIGHTS, AMONG THESE ARE LIFE, LIBERTY
AND THE PURSUIT OF HAPPINESS, THAT
TO SECURE THESE RIGHTS GOVERNMENTS
ARE INSTITUTED AMONG MEN, WE...
SOLEMNLY PUBLISH AND DECLARE, THAT
THESE COLONIES ARE AND OF RIGHT
OUGHT TO BE FREE AND INDEPENDENT
STATES...AND FOR THE SUPPORT OF THIS
DECLARATION, WITH A FIRM RELIANCE
ON THE PROTECTION OF DIVINE
PROVIDENCE, WE MUTUALLY PLEDGE
OUR LIVES, OUR FORTUNES AND OUR
SACRED HONOUR.

THOMAS JEFFERSON
1743 — 1826

IN THIS TEMPLE
AS IN THE HEARTS OF THE PEOPLE
FOR WHOM HE SAVED THE UNION
THE MEMORY OF ABRAHAM LINCOLN
IS ENSHRINED FOREVER

Fifty years after Lincoln's assassination in 1865 at Washington's Ford's Theater (overleaf), it was decided that a memorial to the sixteenth President should stand at the west end of the Mall. Designed by Henry Bacon in 1911 and opened in 1922, the white neoclassical building (above) enshrines Daniel C. French's huge, thoughtful statue of Lincoln (left). Carved on the walls are the words of this revered President's Gettysburg Address and Second Inaugural Address. The design's simple strength and dignity exemplifies the solidarity of the Union, which the nation owes to the man who guided the North to victory in the Civil War. In its commanding appearance, the Lincoln Memorial is also a fitting tribute to the character of the man himself.

Above: the Watergate Complex, the site of the infamous burglary of the Democratic Party's national headquarters in 1972 which led to the first resignation of an American President. Facing page top: the J. Edgar Hoover F.B.I. Building, where 5,000 visitors can be accommodated daily. Now used mainly by the President's staff, the Old Executive Building (facing page bottom) originally housed cabinet offices.

Facing page: the National Shrine of the Immaculate Conception, the largest Catholic church in the country and a masterful adaptation of Byzantine and Romanesque architecture. The Great Dome is covered in a brilliant mosaic depicting the five traditional symbols of Mary; inside there are equally beautiful mosaic reproductions of Titian's "Assumption of the Virgin" and Murillo's "Immaculate Conception." Above: the Latter Day Saints Temple, Kensington, which only Mormans are allowed to enter, and (overleaf) the Church of Mount Saint Sepulcher.

Washington Cathedral (these pages) is a twentieth-century structure built along fourteenth-century lines. It is thought to be the most recent pure Gothic construction in the world. The cathedral's stained glass is particularly impressive; rose windows depict the Creation (top) and the Last Judgement, while in numerous bays stained glass is used in modern and imaginative ways: the George Washington Bay boasts an abstract window by Robert Pinart and another window commemorating the Apollo XI flight contains a sliver of moon rock. Overleaf: fountains colored by spotlights near the Capitol.

The Pavilion Shopping Center, which is situated in the Old Post Office in the Federal Triangle. Once destined for demolition, today the builing contains over fifty shops and food kiosks on its three lower levels which form Washington's newest and most inspired indoor mall – an impulse shopper's paradise. The Old Post Office is easily distinguished on the city skyline since its clock tower is the third tallest structure in the capital.

Left: yellow-painted brickwork and black woodwork are echoed in yellow leaves and black bark in a Washington surburban avenue. Above: the Chesapeake and Ohio Canal, which runs through the heart of Georgetown (overleaf), a Washington suburb that was once an independent tobacco port – so independent, indeed, that when Washington was the capital of the Union, Georgetown was rife with secessionism! Today it is an elegant neighborhood of costly eighteenth- and nineteenth-century homes, many of which have risen in status since their construction – they were built as Irish navvies' cottages. The construction of the C&O Canal was originally advocated by George Washington to bring inland commerce to the city's ports. Eventually built in the nineteenth century, it proved a commercial failure, though the canal is still useful as a recreational facility, being used today for canoeing.

Top: Mount Vernon, the beloved home of George Washington and the place where both he and his wife Martha chose to be buried. Mount Vernon was Washington's favorite estate and, fittingly, it has been preserved today almost exactly as it was in his time. Above, facing page and overleaf: the George Washington Masonic National Memorial, erected by the masonic fraternity of the United States as an expression of their respect for one of their most famous members – Washington took the Presidential oath on a Masonic Bible.

Above left: the slate gravestone and eternally burning flame that mark the final resting place of America's youngest President in Arlington National Cemetery (overleaf). This cemetery is reserved for officers, enlistees and families of the US military and government; American dead of all wars since the Revolutionary War are represented here. The Tomb of the Unknowns (above), which forms the cemetery's centerpiece, contains the remains of servicemen from both world wars and the Korean and Vietnam conflicts. It is guarded day and night by members of the Old Guard, the country's oldest active infantry unit, the twenty-one steps taken by the soldier symbolizing the highest salute. Left: the Arlington Memorial Amphitheater, a 4,000-seat theater that serves as a memorial to the Army, Navy and Marine Corps. Services are held here at Easter, on Memorial Day and on Veterans Day.

The average age of American soldiers in the Vietnam War was nineteen, a youthfulness reflected in a bronze of three servicemen that stands near the wall of names (left) that forms the Vietnam Veterans Memorial. The names of all the men that died in Vietnam are listed in chronological order on these granite panels. All political references are avoided, no ranks are noted – the names alone are a sufficiently eloquent statement on the tragedy of war. Overleaf: the monumental Iwo Jima Memorial in Arlington National Cemetery.

Above and final page: the Washington Monument at sunset, an unmistakable symbol of the aspirations of America, and (overleaf) the Capitol where such ideals confront reality. Facing page: (top) an airliner glides through the dusk on its way to Dulles International Airport, whose striking main terminal building and control tower (bottom) were designed by Eero Saarinen.

125

INDEX